more hallways, Judah fina
placed into Allison's arms.

Allison was too weak to hold Judah on her own, so we propped a pillow under her arm and slid Judah as close to her as possible. She usually had enough strength to hold a bottle and would feed him as often as possible. When she was too tired to continue holding him, she'd turn to me and whisper, "I'm good." Sometimes Allison would just fall asleep holding Judah and the nurse and I would quietly return him to the PICN without disturbing her.

Judah brought his mommy her most peaceful rests. Even in the middle of the night, if Allison had trouble sleeping, the staff would bring Judah for her to hold, and she'd often promptly go to sleep.

In the PICN, Judah received a portion of his donor breast milk from a feeding tube and the other from a bottle as he developed the motor skills to suck and swallow. To accommodate the transition, the feeding tube was removed from his mouth and instead went up his nose and down into his stomach. His small, round face was finally clearly visible.

One day, a mutual friend forwarded Allison and I a message from a woman who had followed our story on social media and felt compelled to pass along information about a financial aid program that her family had been able to take advantage of when her own spouse had been hospitalized. The program was something I had never heard of but was excited to explore. I met with our temporary social worker, Erica, and inquired about the potential aid. Not only was she familiar with it, but Erica was baffled that we hadn't already applied.

"You mean no one told you this program existed until

now?" Erica asked, shocked. She began to explain that if we were approved for it then it could single-handedly wipe out whatever medical bills the insurance didn't cover!

I would have a mountain of paperwork to fill out, but I was hesitant to begin the process since time spent filling out and faxing papers meant time my wife and son didn't have my undivided attention. However, we had amassed more medical bills than we could possibly afford, and we now had a resource I couldn't ignore or put off.

Erica said she had some more good news, but she had to show it to me. As we walked, Erica handed me a large stack of food vouchers for the hospital's cafeteria. "When you need more, just ask me," she said.

The gift overwhelmed me with emotion. Since Allison's admittance to the ICU, my only option for food was in the cafeteria, but I had to pay for everything I ate. I had been deliberately avoiding spending any money, even on food, since my family would be bringing groceries soon and I needed to save as much money as possible.

I held back tears and choked out a soft "Thank you."

Erica took me to a room that had a washer and dryer. There she handed me a gift bag full of laundry detergent. "Same thing applies here. Whenever you need more soap, just let me know and I'll make sure you have everything you need," Erica said.

I was stunned. For months we had family take our laundry back and forth to their homes to be washed for us.

Erica also said, "I don't want to make any promises, but we may have a housing resource for you. It would be off campus but close to the hospital. It's really an apartment complex but you'd have your own room, shower and living area. I'm just confirming a few details."

I cried and hugged Erica. "Thank you so much," I said.

It was amazing how much of a difference one person could make in our lives. In our hometown, several fundraisers were underway, and our community was rallying to help support us financially. Local businesses began to get creative in an effort to aid us even further. A local gym accumulated enough diapers and wipes to last Judah for an entire year, and a real estate company sold over eight-hundred tickets for a dinner fundraiser. Members of our church continued to simply mail us checks to bless us.

A few nurses from hematology stopped by to check on us in the ICU. One of them had accidentally mentioned the surprise baby shower to Allison. She found out the date they had scheduled it for was coming up quickly. Allison was determined to make it back to hematology to enjoy her baby shower with the nurses that had become close friends to her. My days and nights were long and exhausting as I walked back and forth between the ICU and the PICN. The routine quickly became overwhelming as I tried to keep track of their medical progress, be as present for both of them as much as possible and continue the very detailed application process for financial assistance.

While Allison and Judah were technically in separate hospitals, the two buildings were bridged and connected to one another with open hallways. All that separated them was a security guard sitting at a small booth. While staff was allowed to pass freely between the two hospitals, visitors typically were not. Security was aware of my situation and let me pass between the two hospitals by this unconventional route, so I didn't have to walk around the exterior buildings.

One evening, a guard stopped me and demanded to know what I was doing. I showed the guard my pass and explained my situation.

"Who told you could go this way?" He asked.

I named the guard and the director of the PICN who had granted me permission and shared that I had been doing so for some time, but the guard shrugged. "Well, no one told me. You need to go to the front of the hospital, exit there and walk around the block to the front of the children's hospital and enter through the main entrance."

"But....that's the opposite of what I'm allowed to do, sir" I said, baffled.

"I don't care. No one told me and from now on that's the route I want to see you take unless I hear otherwise."

My blood boiled. "Why don't you contact a superior who actually knows what's going on and confirm what I'm telling you."

"Why don't you do what I'm telling you before I have you escorted out of the hospital."

"Look!" I shouted. "I have a wife with leukemia in the ICU and a premature son in the PICN. This route ensures I can spend as much time with both of them as possible. You don't want to do a damn thing that will keep me from either of them or I swear to God you'll be sorry!"

My shouts drew the attention of several onlookers. The guard rose from his booth, but a voice came from behind us before he could do anything.

"He doesn't need to go around."

A PICN administrator that knew me approached the two of us. "Everything he said is correct. Joshua's son is in the PICN and his wife is in the ICU. He has permission to come and go as he pleases. Please ensure the rest of your team is aware of this, officer. Sorry for the miscommunication."

I glared at the guard before leaving and walked alongside the administrator.

"Thank you and... sorry," I said.

"It's alright. I can't imagine what you're going through right now. I'm sorry security didn't know."

I cried. I was disappointed in myself for lashing out. Had the administrator not been present, the guard could've ordered me out of the hospital. My unchecked anger could've forced me away from my family. I could've easily cleared the miscommunication up with a level head and calm demeanor, but I didn't. Even with all that was happening, I had to be better. I couldn't let my emotions dictate my actions. My wife and my son needed the best version of me.

CHAPTER 27

The day for Allison's baby shower came and went while she was still in the ICU. The hematology nurses put her gifts in a safe place until Allison was ready to open them. If her condition improved soon, they'd try and reschedule the party. Allison began short sessions of physical therapy that included standing, sitting up in a chair and, on a good day, taking a few steps. She was exhausted from the effort, but was determined to make progress. When she did manage to sit up straight in a chair, she would continue working on her book.

Several of Allison's toes that had been dark purple turned shades of black as the cells in part of her toes died. A doctor drew short lines with a marker to distinguish where the tips of her toes might have to be amputated.

One night, I began to leave the ICU to go see Judah, but as I rose from where I'd been sitting next to Allison's bed, she grabbed my wrist with surprising force. Allison tried to form words and between heavy breaths said, "Will you...will you please lay down with me?"

I held back tears. Cuddling in her bed was something we had done nearly every night in hematology. During Allison's time in the ICU, we hadn't held one another a single time. The gravity of the isolation and helplessness Allison must have felt alone in that ICU bed really struck me for the first time. While I had done everything in my ability to be present with Allison, I had done little to make her feel like my spouse.

"Yes, of course Allie," I said.

I looked over her body and the bed and wondered if it

was even possible for us to lie down together. Cables and tubes were everywhere. Thick ankle and foot wraps that aided in circulation had been attached her. There wasn't much room.

I turned towards the nurse sitting across from Allison, "Would it be possible for us to be alone for a few minutes?" I asked her.

"Of course," she said standing up. "If you need anything, just call me. I'll wait right outside the door."

Very gently, I helped Allison slide to the edge of her bed and carefully moved her cables and tubes. I had to lay on my side with my butt sticking out over the edge of the bed, but I managed to lay beside my wife. The two of us wrapped our arms around one another. I couldn't even remember the last time we were able to do so.

Allison kissed me gently. "Can you talk to me? It doesn't matter what you say. I just want to hear your voice."

I didn't know what to say. I felt helpless with her so fragile in my arms. Allison was bald, covered in support equipment from head to toe, her belly was swollen from a buildup of fluid, her lungs had a fungal infection, and she was too weak to stand on her own. As Allison's husband, I always felt like I was her protector. How did I protect her from this? I wanted to weep. It felt like I had failed her.

Allison had always enjoyed my singing voice so, instead of speaking, I began to softly sing. I sang about our love and how full Allison made my heart. I sang praises to God for carrying us through a season of darkness and I thanked Him that her physical strength would be restored to match her resilient spirit. I formed spontaneous lyrics about how much I adored life with Allison and any moment spent with her was a fulfilling one that I treasured. I described an adventurous future for myself, Allison, and Judah in New Zealand with rhyming words. No two lines were repeated, and when I finished, I couldn't recall a single thing I had made up.

Tears slowly slid down Allison's cheeks. "That was beautiful," she whispered. "Thank you, baby."

"It's what I'm here for," I whispered back.

I held Allison until she was asleep for several minutes before I rolled backwards off of the bed and quietly put my feet on the floor. I repositioned Allison's sleeping body and slowly made my way out of her room. I thanked the nurse for giving us some privacy and I walked to the PICN to hold Judah.

The next day was September 6 and, even with Allison's continued struggle, it was a day worthy of celebration. It was the day the last of Judah's oxygen support was removed. There were still moments where he held his breath and required physical stimulation to inhale, but it was a huge milestone. The desat episodes would go away over time.

Later that morning, Melissa rolled Judah into Allison's ICU room with a small plastic bathtub, soap, and water. For the first time Allison got to watch Judah get a bath. She smiled as I laid Judah down in a shallow bathtub that caused him to cry.

"He's so cute," she said as I squirted foamy soap on his bottom and back. "Thank you for making this possible," Allison weakly said to Melissa.

"You're very welcome. It's my pleasure," Melissa said, smiling back at Allison.

A freshly washed Judah was then placed in Allison's arms and she fed him a bottle. Judah was visibly growing up and, even in the ICU, it filled my heart to see my wife and son together. Judah stretched out his limbs and one caught on a cable attached to Allison.

"Be careful kid," Allison said, jokingly.

After thirty minutes had passed, she looked at me and smiled, "I'm good."

Melissa and I returned Judah to the PICN.

The next day took a strange downturn for Allison. She began to vomit without warning. A cardiologist entered her room and explained that her heart and kidneys had suddenly started to decline. Excess fluid in her system was putting pressure on her heart which was impaired to the point that it was only beating at a fraction of its capacity. This was making it hard for Allison to breathe and her kidneys were failing to filter fluid out of her body. For the time being, they wanted to move Allison out of the ICU and into cardiology to better care for her heart, which was by far the most pressing challenge she was facing.

In cardiology, a long needle was inserted through the top of her shoulder and a line penetrated her heart. A steroid was administered directly into her heart to keep it beating at a stronger capacity. A thick, cylinder-shaped tube now protruded from Allison's neck in addition to all her other support.

Allison's physical state deteriorated. The woman whom I had embarked on a journey with to the other side of the world just three months before, now needed my help to wipe her bottom. It was a horrible thought but, in some ways, the fragile woman before me didn't feel like my wife anymore. How did our lives change so drastically and so quickly? How did our life go from full of adventure and excitement to fatigue, fear, and disease? Why was God allowing us to go through this?

Erica visited with me and shared the news that I had officially been sponsored to live in an off-campus apartment just a five-minute walk from the hospital. I wept upon stepping into the apartment for the first time. I had a bed, my own shower, and a quiet environment. The administrators of the building had filled the room with baby supplies including a crib, a rocking chair, diapers, blankets, and baby clothes in case Judah was discharged ahead of Allison.

Shortly after the good news about the apartment, Allison's hematology team arrived in her cardiology room and explained that it was time for Allison to have her fifth bone marrow biopsy. I was fearful since I knew her body had endured so much over the last few weeks. Would this test finally reveal the elimination of the leukemia? Was it possible that after all of this treatment any disease could still remain? Could Allison even survive more treatment?

Allison's case was so unique a staff member had asked her permission for her medical records to be available for study. The hematology team had never come across a pregnant woman in her late twenties who had postponed lifesaving therapy to save the life of her unborn child. What would or could happen? It had been expected that Allison would get an abortion and receive her induction chemotherapy right away while she was at her strongest, physically, and mentally. Instead, on top of having acute myeloid leukemia, Allison had undergone two rounds of a weaker chemotherapy treatment and battled the many physical challenges of infections and a weakened immune system. She also had a cesarean delivery and only then received her induction chemotherapy. That treatment was meant to be delivered when you were at your physical peak, not your weakest. Her body was being battered beyond expectation.

Despite the physical pain typically brought on by the bone marrow biopsy, Allison fell asleep before it was finished. Fatigue and sheer exhaustion finally revealed a benefit. It would be several agonizingly long days until the results of the biopsy would be ready. The routine of being monitored, taking medications, examinations, tests and attempts at rest resumed as we waited.

One day, as I fed Judah his bottle in the PICN, my mother kept Allison company in cardiology. She was in the middle of decorating Allison's room with family photos when Allison suddenly spoke.

"Hello?" Allison said.

My mother turned to face Allison and looked around the room thinking someone had entered without her realizing it, but no one else was present. Allison had been in a deep sleep for a little over an hour and, despite speaking, her eyes remained closed. If she was trying to determine if she was alone in the room or not, why wouldn't she just open her eyes? Perhaps she was in a state between dreaming and waking? Her naps were usually interrupted by the frequent traffic of nurses, doctors, and specialists so my mother paused to ensure Allison was actually awake before saying anything.

Allison inhaled sharply, "Hello!" She said.

The change in tone caught my mother off guard. Allison was no longer asking a question...she was making a statement and it was as if Allison was speaking with someone she was excited to see. Did she forget that my mother was with her prior to falling asleep? Who else could she be talking to? My mother watched Allison carefully to see if her eyes were perhaps just slightly open, but after getting closer, she saw that they were indeed closed. Allison was still asleep and obviously dreaming, but that fact didn't lesson the strangeness of her words.

Allison's chin raised as if she were listening to someone speaking and carefully taking in their words. "No," Allison said.

My mother froze, more puzzled than ever.

A long pause, and then Allison stiffened. Once again, she said just one word, "No."

There was a firmness to her tone this time. As if she had disagreed or rejected something. Allison's chest pushed out and very deliberately and even defiantly she said, "It's not time yet."

Allison exhaled deeply and the tenseness in her body completely relaxed. A smile spread across her face.

Allison whispered, "Judah." Her soft smile widened more as she repeated the name of her son, "Judah." Even in her sleep, she radiated happiness, but said no more.

Whatever had transpired in her dreams was now over. Upon waking, my mother and I asked Allison who she had been talking to in her sleep, but Allison had no memory of the conversation or who it was with.

"I wish I knew who I had been talking to," Allison said. "That all sounds so crazy but I don't remember saying any of that."

On September 9, we had some unexpected visitors or, rather...I did. Unbeknownst to me, Allison had coordinated with two women from our church to have a professional family photo shoot. The evening prior to their arrival was the first time

Allison shared the news with me. Even though the photographer was volunteering her time and it was something clearly important to Allison, I was angry. This was certainly not how I wanted our first family portrait to be. I imagined how it would look with Judah having his feeding tube up his nose and Allison half asleep from fatigue and with medical equipment all over her body. I shook my head and grimaced.

I reminded myself to be calm as I entered Allison's cardiology room but what I saw caught me completely by surprise. Allison was sitting up, alert and was applying her own makeup. After days of intense weakness Allison had a second wind of energy. Just the previous night she could barely finish a sentence or keep her eyes open, and now she was smiling and conversational.

"You look beautiful," I said before kissing her.

She ran her fingers through my hair and smiled.

"I'm sorry for being angry last night about the photo shoot. It's important to you and that's all that matters," I said.

"I forgive you," Allison said before kissing me back. "Now Janeen and Elena are going to be here in thirty minutes. You need to get Judah."

"I'm on it," I said, before kissing her once more.

Janeen had been one of our biggest supporters on social media but I had never met her in person. I was curious what she'd be like and how she'd stage us for this unconventional portrait. I made my way down several hallways and passed by a security guard who nodded knowingly at me as I entered the children's hospital. After ringing the buzzer on the door to the PICN, I waited a few moments before a nurse buzzed me inside. I signed in and greeted a few familiar faces as I made my way towards Judah. As I approached his bed I gasped. His feeding tube had been removed! While he still had a few monitors attached to him, the last of Judah's support was gone. I instinctively picked Judah up and held him close to me. With Judah untethered from the shorter tubes, I was able to carry him while I walked around the room. It was a good feeling.

On this day, Allison had been filled with renewed energy and Judah was free of medical support for the first time in his life. I explained the uniqueness of the circumstances to Janeen upon meeting her in person as she mounted a lens to her camera. She began to cry and shared that God had put it on her heart to do the photo shoot that day and now she knew why.

Judah was rolled into cardiology by a nurse and my family, and I spent the next thirty minutes laughing, cuddling, and smiling. Judah was more playful than ever. It was as if he knew he was finally free of tubes and IVs and was loving every minute of it. Allison and I basked in complete adoration of our son and seeing him healthy and strong filled our hearts with a joy we both had been missing for some time. Allison's laugh made me smile so much my cheeks began to hurt.

"Seeing him like this," Allison paused as she gazed at Judah, "just makes this whole crazy journey worth it. Just look at him. He's amazing."

Janeen posed Judah in adorable ways that filled the room with audible "Awwws" from everyone present. She brought a small basket and props to minimize the hospital look of our setting. When we finished, Allison gave Judah one final kiss on the cheek before turning to me and saying, "I'm good."

For a while, we had forgotten we were still in a hospital.

It wasn't until we were done, and I had laid Judah back in his bed for his trip to the PICN, that I noticed something. As the weeks had passed and Judah had more and more support removed from him; Allison simultaneously had more and more support added to her. As I looked at Judah's body without the IVs once taped to his arm, the CPAP that had once pressed against his face, the nasal cannulas and tubes that had gone down his throat and up his nose, I thought to myself that he had been set free from all of it. As I stared at Allison, covered almost head to toe in equipment, I imagined that she had relieved Judah of the heaviness he had once carried. It was as if Allison had taken the burden of all her son's medical needs and placed them on herself.

CHAPTER 28

For the fourth time, my financial aid application was returned with a notation that information was missing and it was unable to be processed. I sighed in frustration because what the letter claimed was missing had never been asked for in the original application. I grabbed a thick folder of documents from my room and set out to scan more papers and fax additional information with the hope that everything would finally be processed this time.

After I finished faxing everything, I entered Allison's room, where she was sitting up and journaling. She closed her notebook upon seeing me and smiled.

"I had a dream," she said.

"Who was it about?" I asked.

Allison would still have the occasional prophetic dream and I assumed she dreamt of someone we knew or one of the medical staff.

"Us," Allison answered.

Allison was still in a weakened state and spoke slowly as she recounted the dream. She dreamt she was in labor. Everything seemed typical of a healthy, natural delivery. Allison pushed and ground her teeth and then Judah was born. We all cheered, laughed, and cried as Judah was put into my arms.

"There's more," the delivery doctor said.

Allison's belly contracted and she began to push again. She gave birth to another child, and then another. In the dream Allison gave birth to three children, but when she awoke, she couldn't remember the gender or names of the last two babies.

In the past, Allison had received several prophetic words that she was going to be pregnant with twin girls one day. A thought had plagued her that when she had miscarried, she had actually lost the twins God had promised her.

She was quiet for a while as she sat on her hospital bed and then shared that she believed the dream of giving birth to three children was prophetic.

"I know Judah's going to be just fine," Allison said. "There's not a doubt in my mind. I also think we're going to continue to grow as a family and have more kids."

For Allison, her dream wasn't just a confirmation of an old promise, but a declaration of life. It was a war cry that she would survive this fight, reclaim her health and we would expand as a family.

Allison changed topics abruptly and said she'd requested to get a feeding tube. They'd be putting it in later that morning. While she had started physical therapy again and was managing to keep some food down, she just wasn't getting the nutrients she needed. A feeding tube had been presented as an option shortly after Allison was admitted to Stanford, despite her being capable of keeping food down at that time. Months later, her scenario had greatly changed but the option for a feeding tube was never presented again, since it had been noted in her medical chart that she didn't want one. Although reluctant, Allison had now decided it was needed. Judah also had an MRI scheduled that morning, so the day was becoming full.

I left Allison to accompany Judah for his MRI and followed him into a small room with a massive MRI machine. He was placed in a small, tight, plastic container and slid into the machine. Judah was made cozy but almost a little too cozy for my own comfort since the tight space and enclosed area was a perfect stage for a SIDS (Sudden Infant Death Syndrome) disaster. Judah wore small yellow earmuffs, while I had ear plugs, to cancel out the blasting noise the MRI made. I remained close to Judah while the nurse waited by the technician. During the thirty-minute test, I continually prayed for grace and protection over him while the machine roared.

Just as Judah finished the last scan, he held his breath and the monitor attached to him blared loudly with red numbers flashing. He was experiencing a major desat. I reached in and vigorously rubbed and stimulated him to get him to take a breath. After two or three unbearably long seconds, he inhaled. His nurse ran towards the MRI table and looked Judah over and the monitors he was connected to.

"Does he have desats?" She asked me.

I looked at her, stunned. "Yes....how could you possibly not know that?" I asked sharply.

Somehow the nurse that accompanied Judah had not been informed of his medical history and had no idea he still held his breath. I was very grateful for the monitor attached to him, because the day could've held a disaster.

After Judah was safely back in the PICN, I returned to cardiology, where a nurse was prepared to insert a feeding tube up Allison's nose and into her stomach. Allison was visibly nervous. As the tube slid up her nose and down her throat, Allison gagged and squirmed while squeezing my hand. The nurse watched a live sonogram that showed the progress of the tube's insertion, but he failed to get the tube where it needed to be. After a few attempts he gave up and another nurse was called in, who succeeded on the first try. The tube went up through Allison's nose and all the way down into her intestine to prevent any strain on her already sensitive stomach.

Tears slid down Allison's cheeks. "I hate this," she said. "How does it look?"

"Silly," I said.

Allison rolled her eyes. "Thanks."

"Can I get you anything?" I asked Allison.

"I just want to take a nap," she answered.

I rose and closed the blinds before giving Allison a kiss and sitting in a chair next to her. After a few short minutes, she was asleep. It wasn't even noon, but it already felt like it had been a long day.

I walked to the PICN and held Judah to my bare chest. A few minutes later my father unexpectedly came in. He smiled and kissed both of us on top of the head.

"Don't you need to be at work?" I asked.

"I wanted to be here today," he answered.

For a moment we sat in silence amongst other sleeping babies and the PICN nurses. Then I began to cry. I was grateful the MRI was over and content to be holding my healthy son in my arms. I was excited for Allison's progress but nervous about the pending results of her biopsy. My conflicted emotions collided. It was too much. Gratitude and concern hit me simultaneously, and I cried over the situation and the many thoughts, concerns and emotions that swirled within me.

My dad leaned forward and wrapped his arms around us.

"I'm sorry, son. I wish I could take this all away from you."

With my son wrapped in my arms and my father's arms

wrapped around me, we sat together and cried.

Later, Nurse Melissa informed us that despite Judah's desats, he was doing very well. It was estimated he'd be discharged before Allison. I knew that the news would be bittersweet for Allison. She would certainly be overjoyed that her son was healthy enough to be discharged, but Allison had long envisioned walking out of the doors of the hospital carrying Judah in her arms when he finally got to leave. Instead, it would have to be in mine until we could leave the hospital together.

On the morning of September 11, my phone rang. A woman introduced herself as a representative from the financial aid program I had applied for. I froze and my heart began to race in anticipation. All of my communication with them had been via letters and this was the first time they had contacted me by phone. The woman informed me that we had been approved! The separate financial aid applications for Allison and Judah had both been approved and whatever medical bills our insurance didn't cover would be completely taken care of by the program. Not only that, but any follow up appointments for either of them over the next year would be covered as well.

For a few moments, I was speechless and couldn't believe what I was hearing.

"Are you there, sir?" The woman asked.

"Yes! Sorry. Ma'am that's...that's the best news I've received in a long time," I said.

The woman went over some details and gave me her information in case I had any questions.

After I hung up, I jumped in the air and shouted, "Yes!"

Knowing there would be no financial responsibilities or

burdens whatsoever was liberating! I thanked God for the friend who had made us aware of the aid, our social worker, Erica, and the people at the financial aid program that had reviewed and approved our application. They had changed our lives!

I told Allison the news and kissed her.

She kissed me back enthusiastically. "Thank you, Jesus!" She said.

My dad rejoiced with us before we sat together and played cards until my mother unexpectedly entered the room. She had left work not long after my father had and the four of us enjoyed each other's company before I left to check on Judah.

Nurse Melissa told me Judah's head physician needed to speak to me. The results of the MRI were in. I fed Judah a bottle until the doctor arrived.

"The MRI showed no abnormalities and Judah's brain looks perfectly healthy," he casually informed me. I kissed Judah as he dozed off, thanking God for a morning of great news!

My mother texted me to head back to Allison's room as soon as I could. Allison's hematology team was coming with the results of her biopsy. I gently set Judah down in his bed and sprinted out of the children's hospital and back to Stanford's cardiology department.

A nurse stopped me just before I entered Allison's room and said a doctor wished to speak with me. She pointed behind me as Allison's lead hematologist approached.

"Hello, Joshua," she said. "Can we talk privately before the team updates your wife?"

I nodded and felt like I was going to vomit. There was no possible way a private talk included good news.

The two of us walked a short distance from Allison's room and the hematologist said, "I apologize for the delay. We took a little longer to get the results because the biopsy showed no residual disease and we wanted to look very carefully to make sure there were no signs of leukemia."

I nodded. "Wait...are you saying the leukemia is gone?"

"Yes," she said.

I stood up straighter and began to tremble and cry.

"I was just speaking to cardiology. They said Allison is expelling fluid from her body and her heart and kidneys are functioning better as well," she continued. The hallway rang with the sound of my hands slapping together. The hematologist smiled, "Things are looking good. I'll be in with the rest of the team in a few minutes to go over what's next, but I thought you should be the one to tell her the news. Congratulations!"

"Thank you! Thank you so much for everything! You and your team! Thank you!" I said and embraced her tightly.

I marched into Allison's room, where she was sitting up with my parents on either side of her. They were all waiting to find out the results of the biopsy.

"No leukemia!" I shouted and raised my arms in the air.

The room was filled with shouts and cries. Allison began to weep and beckoned me to come closer to her. She wrapped her arms around me and sank her head against mine. My tears saturated Allison's cheeks, which I kissed away. My mother sang worship songs, and my father couldn't stop crying. Several times he tried to say something, but simply couldn't put words together because he was so overwhelmed with emotion.

The hematology team entered and elaborated on the good news. In a few weeks, they wanted to repeat the biopsy to confirm the residual disease was still gone. They wanted to give Allison some time for her heart to repair itself before putting her through anything else. As of now cardiology had an expected discharge date for Allison of October 9, just four weeks away. At that point, Allison would be returned to hematology for a few days of observation, followed by the repeat biopsy. She would then begin the process of a bone marrow transplant. With Allison's older sister being a ten for ten genetic match, things looked very promising.

The exact timetable of everything depended on how quickly Allison's heart recuperated, but after the bone marrow transplant, Allison could very well be discharged from the hospital entirely by November, which would be just in time for our eight-year anniversary. It was something to hope and pray for!

We all enthusiastically thanked the hematology team and, after they left, we continued to cry, embrace one another, and sing praises to God. My parents and I gathered around Allison and I prayed, "God, I thank you for this healing and we rejoice in your love and in this celebration. This victory tastes so sweet, Father God, but may this just be the appetizer, and may the main course be on the way."

"Yes, Jesus," Allison whispered.

I quoted Romans 8:36-39, "We face death all day long; we are considered as sheep to be slaughtered. No, in all these things we are more than conquerors through Him who loved us.

For I am convinced that neither life nor death, neither angels nor demons, neither the present nor the future, nor any powers, neither height nor depth, nor anything else in all creation will be able to separate us from the love of God that is in Christ Jesus our Lord."

After I finished praying, my mother asked Allison, "Is there anything we can get you, sweetie? This is a big day so, anything you could possibly want, I'll get for you!"

Allison thought about it. "A pickle. Can I have a pickle? I really want a pickle."

We laughed and my mother left to get Allison a pickle.

I stepped out of cardiology and went into the hospital's chapel, which I had never been in before. It was small, and on one wall was a stained-glass window in three sections. Together they formed a rock with a stream of water flowing into a desert plain. I approached the window, noticing that up close it was actually quite hideous. The texture in the glass had imperfect streaks and it looked messy overall. However, when I backed up the imperfections came together to form a beautiful glass canvas. Whether it was from God or not I'm not certain, but I suddenly had the thought that out of our ugly situation, living waters were going to spring forth. Beauty and life would grow in a place of death. Where I saw trials, disease, and sadness, hope and happiness would spring forth. In that moment, I believed that not only was this battle fought to save Judah's and Allison's life, but something good was going to come out of all this suffering.

I had gone into the chapel to thank God for all the victories we had experienced that day: Allison's leukemia was gone, Judah's MRI scan was normal, and we had received financial aid that would wipe out all of our medical bills. It was a good day, to put it mildly, and yet my thoughts dwelled on the future. I felt compelled to pray for hope for the future and that it would burst forth from a season of hopelessness. Not only for us, but for others who desperately needed hope as well.

As the thought settled in my mind, I felt hands rest on my shoulders. I jumped and looked over my shoulder, but no one was there. Whether it was God's presence, an angel or simply my imagination, I continued to feel hands over each of my shoulders as if to reassure me. It felt good. It felt peaceful.

When I returned to Allison's room a large gift basket was on the counter. It had several goodies for Judah, parking vouchers for the hospital, coffee gift cards and passes for the hospital's cafeteria. There was no card, but a nurse told us our social worker wanted to do something nice for us. I smiled thinking of Erica and how blessed we had been with the men and women who had no doubt been strategically placed in our paths for this journey. We were blessed. Erica had passed our information along to a non-profit organization that gifted us a high-end stroller and car seat for Judah. The day was filled with one precious gift after another! After weeks of low moments and bad news, the day was perfect.

CHAPTER 29

The following morning my parents returned home, and other visitors filled the day. Our friends, the Watsons, returned. David again had his keyboard and set up his instrument in the middle of Allison's cardiology room. Our singing caught the attention of quite a few passing nurses and staff as the sound filled the department. They seemed to enjoy the sound of live music. We sang along to several songs before I received a text message from our friends Mark and Becky who had arrived to visit us as well.

The Watson family said they'd take a little break, but as they prepared to step out, I noticed something strange about Allison's toes. Weeks before, Allison's toes had been dying due to lack of oxygen and her medical team had even drawn lines on them to mark where a possible amputation might have to be made. However, now I noticed that the black and purple colors of dead flesh were receding further away from the lines. Somehow the dead cells were giving way to healthy ones. Was that possible? I pointed it out to everyone as we examined Allison's toes excitedly. I would need to inquire about it with her medical team but, in that moment, it seemed we were witnessing another miracle!

Mark and Becky visited us next and shared photos of their new daughter, Julia, who was born just two days after Judah. Becky was already planning a wedding for our two children! As Allison continued to visit with them, I took Roger, Dahne and David to meet Judah. Over the next few hours, I acted as an intermediary for my wife and son's visitors. I'd take one person at a time into the PICN to visit with Judah, and different groups in to see Allison. The day was full of laughter, singing and sharing life stories. Allison began to tell the Watson family her plans for the future. She intended to return to New Zealand at the earliest opportunity and finish her book. With an incredible testimony to fill her unwritten pages, Allison anticipated her book would tell others of God's faithfulness and act as an example of the miracles He still worked today. She even talked about traveling with Judah as she shared with the world all that God had done in our lives.

Roger recounted all the things that lead up to our relocation to New Zealand and how that in itself was quite a story. With the addition of her battle against leukemia, and Allison's choice to put Judah's life before her own, her story took things to a whole new level.

Roger said, "You had to pass through this for God to elevate your ministry. In order for Him to accomplish what He wants to do through you, you're having to pass through this fire. He's going to take this and elevate you to a place you could never have experienced if it weren't for what's happening in this season." He spoke prophetically to both of us, and it sounded oddly similar to what he had shared with us about the "springboard" back in May, the day we left for New Zealand.

Mark, David, Roger, and I left to get coffee while Becky and Dahne remained with Allison, and planned details of a baby registry for her. With Judah's discharge expected to be soon, we needed some more baby items. Together, they made an online registry and, since Becky was also a new mom, she knew exactly what Allison would need when we left the hospital.

When I returned, I was informed by the ladies that it

was my responsibility to make a flyer to share on social media to promote the baby shower.

"Yay..." I said, sarcastically.

"Hey, we did the hard part and got the registry made already," Becky said.

"And don't buy anything yourselves," Dahne said. "Everyone back home will make sure you have everything you need."

The visit concluded and everyone left for their homes. We were sad to see everyone go, but exhausted from the long day of visitors. Allison hadn't gotten a nap and said she was going to bed early.

Sometime in the night, Allison ripped out her feeding tube. Whether it was done deliberately or in her sleep, she wouldn't say, but Allison refused to have it put back in. An intense fever developed, and she had to receive additional antibiotics as a result. Allison napped frequently the following day and was very quiet. She seemed weaker overall, and when she did want to communicate, she wrote something instead of speaking. I spent nearly the entire morning with Judah and checked in on Allison periodically, but she remained asleep. Her body and mind no doubt needed the rest.

That afternoon I decided to work on the flyer for the baby shower and sat close to Allison as she slept. I had just finished when Allison opened her eyes.

"Hey there," I said.

Allison didn't respond or even acknowledge me. I wondered if she heard me, or in the midst of grogginess even knew I was there.

"Sleep well?" I asked a little more loudly.

Allison looked up and smiled, but not at me.

"Allie?" I asked.

She was either oblivious or ignoring me, but something else had her complete attention.

Suddenly, Allison was beaming. A wide smile spread across her entire face.

"Allison?" I asked, nervously.

Allison's head turned back and forth as well as up and down. Her eyes looked around the room with a sense of wonder and her smile never faded. Small tears began to form in her eyes.

"Allison, please say something," I said, and leaned close to her.

For the first time, she acknowledged me, but with a mere wave of her hand, as if she was waving me off.

I began bombarding Allison with pleas for her attention.

"What are you smiling at? Do you see something? Answer me."

I had no idea what was going on but, despite Allison's happiness, it was terrifying me.

She shook her head and gestured that she wanted to write something. I set a notepad on her leg and placed a pen in her hand.

Clumsily Allison wrote, "Are you done yet?"

I was startled by her curt response and Allison returned to looking around the room.

"Allison, please tell me what's going on!" I said, through tears. Was she hallucinating?

Allison sighed, looked at the pad of paper and began to write again. "Angels," she wrote.

"You see angels right now?" I asked, doubtfully.

Allison stared at me unblinkingly and then wrote, "My angels are so heavenly."

I looked around the room as if I expected to see what she was encountering. I didn't see anything.

"Where?" I asked.

"Angels everywhere," Allison wrote before she returned the pen to me and returned her attention to what she was seeing.

I still suspected she was hallucinating and was about to call a nurse in when I stopped myself. I felt compelled to simply pray. Silently, I asked God if Allison was in any danger, if she needed help and if what she claimed she was seeing was really happening.

In the stillness of the room, I waited and about a minute later I felt God say, "What she's experiencing is very precious. Do not interrupt it."

I began to cry softly, and I quietly picked up my chair and moved into the corner of the room behind Allison. I no longer wanted to be a distraction in any way. There, I watched and waited. My eyes perceived nothing angelic or miraculous, nor did I feel God's presence. However, I knew that was entirely irrelevant. Even if I couldn't detect it with my own senses, something supernatural was happening, and Allison had a front row seat to it.

Minutes later Allison fell asleep again. When she awoke, she had a second wind of energy, but her breathing was labored.

"Hi," I whispered to her.

"Hey," Allison said.

"I'm sorry about earlier," I said.

"It's okay."

"Do you remember what happened?" I asked.

Allison smiled. "I remember everything." I waited for her to elaborate. "There were angels everywhere. They were floating all around the room. They were all singing together it...." Allison smiled to herself as she remembered. "It was the most beautiful sound I've ever heard," Allison said.

"Has anything like that happened before?" I asked.

"No. Never."

"Why do you think it happened now?"

"I don't know."

I wasn't even sure what to ask or say next. What had happened seemed so incredible and yet I had no part in it. It was strange to even try to imagine what Allison had seen.

We sat in silence for a while before I asked, "What were they singing?"

"They were singing glory to God," Allison answered.

We were interrupted before I could ask her any further questions.

Allison's cardiologist entered the room and confirmed that she had an infection of some kind, which was the source of her fevers. Further, fluid was building in Allison's lungs, which explained her labored breathing. Given her counts were stable, Allison's team wanted to attempt to drain the fluid from her body.

"How does that happen?" I asked.

The doctor explained they would insert a long needle through Allison's back and directly into her lungs to draw out the excess fluid with a syringe.

Allison sighed. "How soon?" she asked.

"Within the next few hours," the cardiologist answered.

Allison's friend, Melissa, arrived just prior to the procedure. Melissa proved a delightful distraction for her as she rubbed her dry feet with lotion and painted her nails. The two of them did a devotional together and talked about God's enduring love in hard times. Allison didn't say much during the visit, but it was clear she enjoyed her company greatly.

A doctor entered the room with an assistant and prepared for the procedure. Allison would have to sit up and lean forward for them to withdraw the excess fluid in her lungs, but she was too weak to do that and hold herself up. I stood in front of Allison and held her against me. Melissa slid Allison's narrow meal table between us to take some of the weight off and add stability. It was important that Allison remain as still as possible. The doctor described everything he was about to do before he did it. I rubbed Allison's head and pulled her into me as I watched a long needle pierce her back and move deep into her body. Allison didn't even flinch.

"Do you feel anything?" I asked.

"I feel it, but I'm just so tired," Allison said.

The doctor took a clear, plastic cylinder and attached it to the base of the needle and began to extract fluid out of Allison's lungs. As he did, she began taking deeper and deeper breaths. The doctor watched a screen that displayed Allison's vitals with a careful eye.

The draining continued for a short while before Allison whispered, "Tell them to stop."

"Are you hurting?" I asked.

Allison didn't say anything but nodded slightly.

I bit my lip, unsure of what to do. I knew this was important, but my wife was in pain.

"Are you guys close to being finished? She wants to stop," I said.

"We can stop there," the doctor said. "She did good."

Together, Melissa and I carefully laid Allison back down on her bed. She fell asleep the instant her head touched the pillow. I thanked Melissa for visiting and then, once again, we were alone.

Allison woke up briefly and I tried to convince her to let a nurse replace her feeding tube, but she shook her head defiantly and said, "It's not my responsibility anymore."

I pressed Allison to elaborate on what she meant, but she fell asleep again. I sat by her bed and watched her for a long time before leaving to see Judah.

CHAPTER 30

In the PICN, Judah devoured his bottle in no time and fell asleep against my bare chest. My eyes were closed, but I was wide awake. It had been a full day with all of the staff coming in and out because of Allison's fever. I reminded myself of all the good news we had received over the last few days. Judah could be discharged soon, and Allison had beat her leukemia.

While that was the best news in the world, Allison didn't look like she had won any battle. Months of fighting had left her battered and depleted. The body that had often twirled, leapt, and danced was still confined to a bed. I wanted to scoop Allison up and take her and Judah to Monterey, one of our favorite coastal cities. A family friend had told us they wanted to treat us to a stay at a resort there for a few days. It was quite a gift, and one that Allison and I longed to share together. If we left for Monterey soon after being discharged, it would be our first trip as a family. I couldn't think of a better place to go and celebrate life. The threat of death and darkness had loomed over us for so long, and those clouds were finally starting to break.

"How much longer?" I asked myself. How many more weeks would Stanford be our home? How long would it be until Allison could walk out of those big glass doors carrying Judah? How long before we could finally begin our lives as a family?

There were so many little things I missed: sleeping in a bed with Allison, going for a drive to get coffee, playing video games together, or even just sitting beside one another reading. No doubt, the dynamic of everything was about to shift with Judah in our lives, but for years we had wanted a child and now he was finally here. Our most precious gift was in my arms, asleep against me.

"Mommy can't wait to come here again and hold you," I whispered. "This will all be over soon. You're going to love New Zealand, buddy."

It was getting late, and I knew I needed rest. I rose and laid Judah down in his bed. He didn't even stir from the movement. After gently kissing him on the head, I whispered "Goodnight, my son. Love you lots."

The long hallways in the hospital were empty. As I stepped outside, a cool breeze enveloped me, and the sounds of the trickling water fountains filled the air. The walk back to the apartment felt long. As the elevator took me to my floor, I had trouble keeping my eyes open. Inside my room, I contemplated just jumping in bed, but I typically slept better after a shower. I pulled my shoes and socks off and was just about to remove my shirt when the phone rang.

"Who could be calling me this late?" I said out loud.

I pulled my phone out of my pocket and read the caller ID which displayed a Stanford number.

I answered the phone, "Hello?"

"Is this Joshua Cordero?" A woman's voice said.

"Yes, who is this?" I asked, suddenly worried about Judah.

"Joshua, I'm calling about your wife, Allison."

I stood up and my heart began pounding so loud I strained to hear the woman's words. "Yes?" I asked.

"Are you still in the hospital?" She asked.

"No, but I'm close," I said.

"You need to get here right away," the woman said.

I had trouble forming my next words, "Is she...okay?"

"Allison's blood pressure just crashed, and she doesn't have a pulse. We're trying to revive her now."

It felt as if my heart was about to launch out of my chest. I sprinted towards the door and out of the apartment.

"Is she going to die?" I asked, instinctively.

There was a pause as I reached the elevator. "Get here as soon as you can," the woman said.

"I'm coming," I said, before I hung up and entered the elevator.

The elevator descended agonizingly slowly. My foot tapped nervously on the floor as I waited.

"Please, God. Fight for her. Save Allison," I spoke pleas and prayers. "Don't let this be the end."

The elevator reached the bottom of the first floor and I ran through the lobby and back outside. If only I had stayed with Judah a few more minutes, I would've still been in the hospital when they called. As soon as I began running down the road, I cursed myself. In my haste to get out of the apartment I had grabbed sandals instead of putting my shoes back on. The loose straps caused the sandals to slide back and forth as I ran, slowing me down. Loud slaps filled the air as the rubber collided with concrete and asphalt. I couldn't get my body to go as fast as I needed it to, and everything seemed to move torturously slow. I screamed out loud as I pumped my arms and legs to move down the sidewalk and to the hospital. The entire distance from my apartment to cardiology was a little over half-a-mile. Would Allison still be alive by the time I arrived in her room?

The streets were empty as I sprinted. I pushed myself harder and harder to move as fast as I could as I approached the building. I ran past the water fountains and neared the main entrance.

"Almost there. Almost there," I said to myself. "Keep going! Faster, dammit!"

The glass doors slid open slowly and I nearly smashed into them. My sandals slid on the recently cleaned floor. Only one long hallway remained before I'd reach cardiology. I gasped for air as I kept running.

"Please be alive. Please be alive," I kept thinking over and over.

I turned a corner, racing past the chapel where I had thanked God for the defeat of Allison's leukemia just two days before, and then crossed into the cardiology department. After a sharp left turn, I saw Allison's room. The door was open. I burst inside, stopping suddenly. The room was filled with people. Over a dozen men and women surrounded Allison.

"I'm her husband!" I shouted.

Every head looked up for a moment and a few people stepped aside for me to get to Allison. I still couldn't see her and had no idea if she was even still alive. A nurse took a step backwards and I finally saw her. Allison's eyes were wide and darted to meet mine. She raised her hand and wrapped her fingers around my own. I fell to my knees and our foreheads touched.

"I'm here," I said.

"You're here," Allison said as she closed her eyes.

She was a mess. Tubes and cables were everywhere.

Her gown was ripped open, and she had drops of blood all over her. Nurses and doctors moved back and forth around her bed. I just held Allison's hand and told her I loved her. Allison opened her eyes and winced at a bright light that was shining in her face.

"Can you turn that light off, please?" She asked.

Someone in the room said, "We need to see what we're doing, sweetie."

Allison was annoyed. "I want to go back to sleep," she said.

The same person said, "Allison, your heart stopped beating a little while ago. We need a few minutes to make sure you're okay."

Allison rolled her eyes, "You said that a few minutes ago." My wife looked at me. "I'm sick of being here."

"I know. We'll be in Monterey before you know it," I said.

In an attempt to distract her, I asked, "What happened? Do you remember anything?"

She thought about it before she answered and said, "I just remember feeling funny and then everything went dark. I... I woke up and there were so many people. I shouted, 'I'm here!' I feel fine now."

"Did they have to resuscitate you?" I asked.

The moment I asked the question I knew how absurd it sounded. How would Allison even know?

A nurse next to me said, "They barely started before her pulse came back."

"Well, there you go," Allison said.

I smiled at my wife and kissed her hand. "Were you scared?" I asked Allison.

My wife looked at me for a few seconds before she answered, "A little, but only because you weren't here."

I held back tears as guilt washed over me. "I'm so sorry I wasn't here, Allie," I said.

"It's okay. I'm not mad or anything. It was just scary not having you with me."

One by one, the doctors and nurses began to leave Allison's room. When I attempted to get answers as to what happened, a nurse repeated what the woman on the phone had told me earlier. Allison's blood pressure abruptly plummeted and then she had no pulse. However, no one could really say how or why that had happened.

"You mean you have no idea why she almost died tonight?" I asked.

"We'll run some tests but, as of now, we don't know," he said.

The situation was as baffling as it was frustrating. Allison's leukemia was gone. A discharge date was on the calendar. The worst was supposed to be over. What was going on?

I spent the night in Allison's room, but barely slept. In the morning, more tests took place, including blood cultures, CT scans and x-rays. Foot traffic was once again busy, but we still had no answers. My father and Allison's mother came to the hospital. The day seemed to move so slowly as we waited and watched for Allison to improve.

The following day was September 15, 2015. When I arrived in Allison's room, my father was already there playing a game of cards with her. Her face and body seemed very fatigued. Her breathing was labored, and her belly was swollen again.

I had just joined in on the card game when a nurse entered. It was a woman I had never seen before.

"You're the husband?" She asked me.

"Yes, ma'am" I said.

"Could we step into the hallway for a moment?" The nurse asked.

I was puzzled. "Is it about Allison?" I asked.

"Yes, we have some updates."

"Well, if it's about her, you can share it with both of us," I said.

The nurse's eyes shifted from me to Allison and back. Allison was still focused on the card game and didn't seem to notice or care.

"It's about her counts."

I paused waiting for her to elaborate. The nurse seemed impatient.

"It might be better if we spoke in the hallway," she repeated.

I sighed and followed her out of Allison's room.

"We've had to increase your wife's adrenaline to a very high dosage. Her heart is beating at about fourteen percent of its capacity and..."

"Wait...what?" I cut the nurse off.

"Allison's lead cardiologists and her primary hematologist would like to speak with you."

I was stunned. "Is she...dying?" I asked.

"Her team will be able to give you more information," the nurse said. "If you can wait in the conference room, they'll join you in just a few minutes."

"Okay..." was all I could say.

The woman left me alone in the hallway. I looked through the window into Allison's room. She and my father continued to play cards. I opted to wait until I talked to Allison's team before sharing anything with either of them. Instead, I texted Allison's mother and asked her to join me in the conference room. The two of us sat at the long table and I began scribbling down questions to ask the team when they arrived. My mind wandered to dark conclusions of what they might say, but I reminded myself of all God had done to lead us to this point. There was no possible way Allison's journey would end in Stanford.

CHAPTER 31

Sharon and I waited for a few minutes before half a dozen people filled the room, including Allison's social worker, her lead cardiologist, and her primary hematologist. I had never seen these individuals together in one setting before. My heart began to beat quickly.

The cardiologist sat across from me and started to share an update, "The cardiology team has been monitoring Allison for several weeks, ever since her heart function declined in the ICU. She was brought here because the dominant problem was her heart. We've been doing everything we can with heart medicines to sustain her and remove as much of the fluid as possible that she has been retaining, to try and assist the kidney function and help give her every chance to recover. We knew from the beginning that the type of injury her heart has is from the chemotherapy. We can't say that with one hundred percent certainty, but it's most likely. While there can be some recovery with the severity of the injury she has, the likelihood of substantial recovery is low. We wanted to give her every possible chance."

The doctor paused to give us a moment to absorb what he was saying before continuing. I had never been told the severity of her heart's impairment until then. Did they think Allison ever had a real chance of returning to hematology for her bone marrow transplant?

"As you know, the last few days Allison's been going downhill again. On top of everything she has, there is another severe infection, the source of which is not clear... It's been very difficult for her body to handle it, despite very aggressive attempts on our end to help her. Now, Allison's breathing is more labored, which is expected because she's retaining fluid again."

A lump formed in my throat and my mouth was suddenly dry. I thought of Allison's swollen belly.

The cardiologist said, "We did an ultrasound of her heart early this morning to see if there had been any recovery since her admission to cardiology. She's been on a lot of medicine. High dosages of adrenaline. Despite all of this, the ultrasound showed her heart is even worse than before."

In my peripheral vision, I glanced over at Sharon. She was composed, but I could tell she was holding back a lot of emotion. We were hearing the worst possible news about the woman we loved the most.

The cardiologist continued, "She also has a very large blood clot in her heart which, quite honestly, is normal given all that she's sustained. Her blood is stagnant and isn't moving the way it should be. It's a sign of just how bad her heart is, really. We had very much hoped to see improvement in terms of the capacity of her heart recovering, but being this far out, and the heart's functioning still being this low...any hope of a meaningful recovery is essentially near zero. I wish I had other news to report."

My head hung low, and I wanted to crumple up the paper I was holding with the questions I had written down. I wanted to march into Allison's room and carry her out of the hospital, put her into a vehicle, and drive to Monterey with her.

Allison's hematologist weighed in and emphasized that even if we hadn't gone through with the last treatment,

Allison's leukemia would still be present and would most likely kill her within weeks. He had redirected any blame that might have been put on hematology as the culprit for Allison's impaired heart, but the truth was I didn't blame them in any way. He was right. Allison had chosen to go against their medical advice for the sake of prioritizing Judah's health and wellbeing over her own. The treatment had worked, but with all Allison had chosen to do prior to that, including two other rounds of chemotherapy and giving birth, the result was more bitter than sweet. With the combination of several physically demanding treatments, a rare and deadly disease, a major surgery and now several infections, Allison's body was broken and could tolerate no more.

I asked redundant questions and had them clarify and elaborate on what had happened to lead us to this, even though I already knew the answers. My mind didn't quite believe what I was hearing.

"Can anything else be done for her heart?" I asked.

"No," the cardiologist said. "We've been giving her heart every possible chance to recover. What's happening now is her other organs are in the process of getting worse and starting to shut down. She's made very little urine today because her kidneys aren't functioning properly since they're not getting blood. The results of her liver tests are going the wrong direction, and I suspect they'll continue to do so. Her breathing is becoming more labored, and I think we're going to find her lungs filling with more and more fluid. We're not withholding anything that we can bring forth. There just isn't a realistic possibility of recovery." The doctor was blunt, but solemn as he continued, "My worry is that with the events of the last forty-eight hours, she will continue to get worse quickly. Allison's heart is working at only fourteen percent of its capacity. She's on the highest dosages of her medicines. The one thing we can do for her at this point won't change the fundamental outcome, but rather focus on her not suffering at the end. No matter what we do, her time is very short. I think likely even hours to days, not weeks to months."

The room fell silent and suddenly felt very stuffy. I wanted to throw something and scream. The reality of how much time Allison had left was impossible to accept. Just four days before, we had celebrated that she was leukemia free and had a discharge date on the calendar. I asked about extracting the fluid that had built up in Allison's body and if that could help as it had before.

The Cardiologist answered, "No. When the body doesn't get enough blood moving, acid builds up in the body and people have to breathe faster and that gets tougher and tougher to do. I think we'd be causing her more discomfort than relief. In the state that she's in now, putting her on a breathing machine, giving her chest compressions, shocking her heart, would just needlessly put her through pain at the end. I'd focus on things that would keep her comfortable."

"I think she's alert enough to make her own decision," I said.

"I understand," the doctor answered. "I would encourage you to frame it to her that...we've already been artificiality supporting her for some time now."

Despite the truth of his words, I hadn't thought of it that way until that moment. Allison was only alive because of the adrenaline and medicine being fed directly into her heart and even that was failing her.

"We can certainly tell her what we've shared with you," the cardiologist said.

"Thank you, but I want to tell her myself."

"There is some relative time urgency to make decisions about things. This scenario could come up tonight or even this afternoon." He sighed as sadness hung over his face. "I am sorry. I am so sorry about everything. This is a terrible thing to go through and I wish we could do more," he said with deep sincerity.

I sat and absorbed everything for a few moments. I didn't know what else to say.

Finally, I broke the silence and said, "Thank you. I know everyone did their best."

I scanned each of the faces of the people I had come to know well over the previous few months. Talented, kind, and dedicated men and women. People that had fought with all of the best treatments, knowledge and resources modern medicine could offer, and yet it wasn't enough. However, there were times when it hadn't been enough before. I remembered when we were told Allison would most likely perish giving birth to Judah and how physically fragile our son would be. Everyone was wrong. Could they be wrong again? Was this a time to prepare for the inevitable, or hope for a miracle?

"You all did your best," I said again. "When Allison was first diagnosed, she had chosen to postpone the most effective treatment because she wanted to save her son. She knew there were major risks." However, Allison's choices were no longer risks, they were consequences. I shook my head in disbelief. "Thanks for your time," I said.

Our social worker approached me and mentioned that there was an art package the hospital had that Allison could use to place her handprint on a piece of parchment next to Judah's handprint. The concept was to have a memento of mother and son's handprints alongside one another. I gratefully accepted the offer and made my way out of the conference room and into Allison's room.

A nurse and my father were with Allison.

"Can you give me some privacy with Allison, please?" I asked.

My dad didn't seem to think anything of it and quickly stood up from his chair.

"Of course," the nurse said.

They both left the room, and Allison and I were alone. I took my time and relayed all that Allison's team had shared with me. Allison stared at me intently through deep breaths. When I finished, she said nothing.

"What are you thinking?" I asked her.

"I'm walking out of here...carrying Judah," Allison said defiantly. "I don't...I don't care what they say."

There was no sadness, acceptance or even tears from Allison, just resistance and confidence. I kissed her deeply. The two of us prayed and discussed what to do, medically, even in the unlikeliest of outcomes. I mentioned the handprints idea to Allison, and she wanted to do it.

"I want to take a nap first, though," she said. I stood up and Allison held up her hand to stop me. "Give me a piece of paper."

I knew what it was for and brought Allison paper and a pen. While we had missed days off and on, Allison continued to fill her vases with notes about what she was praying for, what she was grateful for and what she planned to do when she was discharged.

"Can you write for me?" Allison asked.

"What am I writing?"

"For the prayer vase write, 'A new heart.'"

Tears formed in my eyes as I wrote the date and the words she told me to. I wrote out what Allison was grateful for and what she wanted to do when she was discharged and placed the three papers in their designated vases.

As I left Allison's room, my dad approached me. He was weeping and he grabbed me in a bear hug. Sharon had told him everything. I held him for a while before letting go.

"I'm going to go see Judah," I said.

Allison's younger sister, Marisa, and my mother drove to Stanford as soon as they heard the news. My sister, Kelly, booked a flight from her home in Texas to San Francisco. Everyone had prepared for the worst. All there was left to do was wait and see if we'd experience another miracle.

I didn't know what to do with myself. Since our supernatural encounter at Bethel Church, we had experienced one incredible or miraculous encounter after another. Even through the onset of disease and the threat of death, we had pressed on. Was this a time to accept defeat or continue to have faith? That choice was Allison's alone and she wanted to keep fighting. In my heart, I knew I loved a God who still performed miracles. I had seen plenty of them myself. Healing Allison was certainly not outside of His reach. Was it possible a great miracle would happen in the eleventh hour? Allison seemed to think so.

I made my way to the third floor of the hospital, where the main building branched off from cardiology and turned toward it. There I found myself looking out a window on the third floor that peered down at Allison's own room on the first floor. Her blinds were open, but I couldn't see inside. Construction was going on outside and the only view from Allison's room was dirt and construction equipment. Did Allison really go from living in New Zealand and having some of the best views in the world to dying in a hospital room with a view of a construction site? She was only twenty-nine and had just had her first child. Her whole life should still be ahead of her. I could not come to any conclusion of how or what to think, nor did I hear or feel anything from God as I prayed and prayed for a miracle. I dropped to my knees and cried softly in front of the window. My hand touched the glass and reached towards Allison's room.

"Don't let this be the end," I whispered. "Let me walk into her room and she's sitting up, breathing normally. You've given us miracles before, now do it again. You brought us to the opposite side of the world and back. We followed You every step of the way. We surrendered everything just as You asked us to. Allison fought for her son. Now, please God...fight for Your daughter. Don't abandon her to death. I know You've been a part of this journey. Please don't leave it now."

I turned and saw that down the hall my parents were standing together, watching me. We met each other halfway, embraced and cried.

"I'm sorry you're both having to go through this, my son," my mother said. "We're still praying for her."

A few minutes later, a nurse, Judah and I made our way

to Allison's room. As the three of us turned into cardiology and neared Allison's room, I still hoped we would enter and see Allison sitting up, smiling, and that I would witness yet another miracle. Instead, when we entered, I fought the urge to cry as I saw Allison wearing an oxygen mask. Instead of energetic, she looked more exhausted than ever.

Allison and Judah had their hands placed onto an ink pad and then onto a slip of thick paper. When they were finished, Allison asked to hold her son. Judah slept in her arms while I wrapped my arms around both of them. We didn't say anything. Allison lovingly watched Judah, and eventually fought to keep her eyes open.

She looked at me, nodded, and whispered, "I'm done."

My heart sank. Every single time when Allison was content with her time with Judah, she would say the phrase, "I'm good." Why did she say, "I'm done"?

Judah was returned to the PICN, but I remained with Allison and was eventually joined by my parents, Sharon, and Marisa. Kelly was still on her way from Texas. It started to get dark as we all sat together quietly. Allison began doing some of her stretching exercises and extended her arms in different directions. As she lifted her hand one of her fingers caught the tube that went through her neck and fed adrenaline directly into her heart.

Allison winced.

I leaned toward her and asked, "Are you okay?"

She raised her index finger and bent it down and up twice.

She was breathing even heavier and seemed very uncomfortable. I had a thought, but wanted to share it privately with Allison, so I asked everyone to leave. Out of the many instruments attached to Allison, the large tube coming out of her neck was by far the most uncomfortable for her. It was essentially keeping her alive, however, the medical staff had just told me that morning that it was no longer enough.

"Do you want it removed?"I asked her.

I wasn't ready to accept death any more than Allison was, but if this was indeed the end, I wanted her to be comfortable in her last moments. With it gone, maybe in the unlikeliest of hours we would finally see God perform a miracle in Allison's heart. Allison understood what I asked and nodded. If God was going to do something, this was the moment for it to happen.

We prayed together and I called a doctor inside. I shared that Allison wanted her adrenaline removed.

The doctor nodded and looked at Allison, "You understand that if we remove it, though, you'll die very quickly?"

Allison's breathing was so labored, we couldn't tell if she had nodded or not.

"Allison?" I asked. The doctor and I leaned into Allison and her eyes were only partially open. "Allison, can you hear me?" I asked louder. My heart began to pound. "Allie? Please answer me baby!" I said, desperately. I looked at the doctor who frowned at me sadly.

"Would you like me to get the rest of your family?" he asked.

I gasped at the request and tears began to stream down my face. I nodded. Allison's eyes widened and her lips parted, but she didn't say anything. Her monitor began to beep frantically. If she was going to speak, there was no way I was going to be able to hear her.

"Can someone turn that machine off!" I shouted.

A man entered the room, apologized, and pressed several buttons until the sounds were muted. Allison was surrounded by all five of us. She stared into my eyes and I brought my face close to hers. Allison searched my face and her lips parted once again but no words came out. Her teeth ground together. She seemed to be struggling to say something but was unable to. An unnatural sound escaped from her mouth and in that moment, I knew she was dying. I kissed Allison's lips softly, but she did not return the kiss. My dad stepped away from the bed and began to cry.

"Allison, don't go," I said, and started to weep. Through tears and whimpers I said, "You have to stay here with me. You have to help me raise our son. Stay with us. Please."

Allison broke eye contact with me and her chin rested on her chest. Every breath she took was deep and strained with difficult effort, as her body began to betray her.

Marisa told Allison she loved her.

Sharon said, "I love you, Allison. You're the best daughter I could've ever asked for."

Instinctively, I grabbed Allison's phone and resumed playing the last worship song she had played. It was "All Hail" by Daniel Bashta. Soft music filled the room, followed by the words:

> My God, my rock, a mighty fortress
> Strong to deliver and rich in love
> I stand in awe of all Your promises
> And all Your justice true

my heart will trust in You

All hail King Jesus, all hail our God Emmanuel
Rejoice, let every voice sing Yours is the kingdom forever

We worship the Lion, we worship the Lamb
All praises belong to the One who was slain
We worship our warrior we crown You as king
Satan's defeated, he's under our feet

My mother had opened her Bible and was reading out loud the account of Jesus healing Jairus' daughter. The words of a miraculous encounter between Jesus and a dying girl filled the room. Even in that moment of terror, I knew Allison could also sit up, stand up and walk around completely healed.

I began to pray, but Allison was fading.

"Allison, you need to finish your story. It's not supposed to end here! It ends with you walking out of this place holding Judah! Remember? That's what you said! You're not dying here. You're going back to New Zealand with me and we're having more babies just like you dreamed! Allison!" I cried.

Allison didn't respond. The pause between her breaths was now extending. Her eyes were closed and each time she inhaled her breath was filled with short gasps. Allison's chest was only barely rising. Dread fell over the room. I continued to cry out to God and Allison, through sobs and tears. My hope dwindled into shock and disbelief. My wife was fading before me, in my very arms. I shook her gently, but she didn't move.

"Allison?" I asked.

She was no longer noticeably breathing. I checked Allison's neck for a pulse but couldn't feel anything. I cried out for a doctor and the one I had spoken to earlier rushed in with a stethoscope and placed it against Allison's chest. He listened carefully for several seconds and looked at me sadly.

"I'm very sorry," he said.

I opened my mouth to say something, but only a painful moan came out. I had heard accounts before of peace in the midst of a loved one dying. A warm assurance that they were no longer hurting and had gone on to be with their Heavenly Father, but I felt no peace and no assurances of any kind in that moment. If God was in the room, He was silent, and His presence was not felt. Instead, I felt despair that was so suffocating I could not breathe.

My moans turned into screams, as I was submerged in absolute agony. It felt as if my heart had been torn out of my chest and I had been cast into an ocean of loss and torment. No miracles manifested. All thoughts and feelings were abandoned, and only pain remained. My hope for a miraculous healing had been struck down, along with the precious life that had once resided in the body that I held close and wept over. The rooms and halls of the hospital echoed with the cries of a broken man, who had lost the love of his life and whose faith had been betrayed.

Allison would never walk out the doors of the hospital like she had declared. She could no longer pen a story of healing and restoration like she had expected. Her dreams of returning to New Zealand, raising her son, and having more children would never be realized because she was a part of this world no longer.

Allison Victoria Cordero was dead.

CHAPTER 32

For hours I wept at Allison's side. I could feel her once warm body turn cold, and her soft skin become stiff. Her complexion had already changed. She didn't even look like Allison anymore.

How had it come to this? Was this the reward of faith? Allison and I had walked in such a deeply intimate place with Jesus for over a year-and-a-half. We had been part of incredible miracles. We had heard the voice of God encourage us and direct us. What was the point? If this was the end of the journey, why did God even bother telling us to take the first step? Was this the reward for surrendering all to Him? It felt like God had betrayed our trust, our love, and our relationship with Him. He had abandoned us in our most desperate hour.

Slowly, I pulled away from Allison's body and paced around the room. I looked at the scores of photos that were on the walls. Images that chronicled our journey. I stared at pictures of Allison and I filming and traveling together.

"Why?" I said out loud. "Why? Why? Why?"

My sister entered the room. She had arrived from Texas but was too late. Kelly looked at me and then to Allison. "Oh...oh no," she said through tears. She gently cupped Allison's cheek in her hand. Kelly absorbed the shock and sadness of Allison's death and then approached and embraced me. The two of us cried as we held one another.

Each of us had a moment alone with Allison and said our goodbyes. I walked down the long hallway to the PICN and approached Judah's bed. Three nurses were in the room. While none of them approached me, they all watched with sad faces. I assumed they were aware that my wife had just died. I stared down at my son, who was sleeping so peacefully. He had no idea or concept of what had transpired. I cried as I realized that Allison would never get to hear Judah say, "Mommy." Judah would never get to play with Allison, or have any memories of her. Allison's dream of swinging Judah back and forth between us as waves crashed over his feet would never come to pass. Allison had said many times she wanted to teach Judah to dance. More than anything, she couldn't wait to dance and worship with him. A dream that would never be realized. The mother who loved her child more than her own life and longed to be a parent more than anything in the world would never truly get to experience motherhood.

I'm not sure what compelled me to do so, but in that moment, I began to thank God for Judah's health and his life. My gratitude suddenly caught in my throat as I thought I heard Allison's voice. Then I realized I was still hearing it. My heart raced for a moment and I turned around.

Perhaps God had raised Allison from the dead. My hope soared, but then it sank just as suddenly. Allison was not in the room, and I realized what I had heard. On the corner of Judah's bed was an mp3 player playing a recording of Allison talking to Judah. In case Allison had a rough day of recovery, she had decided to make a recording of herself reading stories, praying, and telling Judah how much she loved him so he could still hear her voice even if she couldn't be physically present with him. It was playing on a loop. The recording would be the only bedtime stories and prayers Judah would get to experience with his mommy.

I sighed and rested my cheek against Judah's.

"I love you, Judah. I love you so much. Mommy loves you so much."

I stayed with Judah for a while and then returned to cardiology. Everyone was waiting outside Allison's room. I went inside and sat beside Allison's body once more. On her lap was the teddy bear she had received from City Impact Church, when she was first hospitalized in New Zealand.

The corpse next to me was not how I remembered Allison. The pale, hairless, and swollen body was a poor imitation of the vibrant, loving, strong and fearless woman that I loved with all my heart, and yet I spoke to Allison's body.

"I want you back," I said. "Come back. In Jesus' name, come back."

I waited, but Allison's motionless body remained still. I let out a long sigh. Anguish filled my body and spirit. Had Allison and I been faithful or naive this whole time? I felt like I was drowning, but had no idea how to pull myself above the water to gasp for air. There was a primal need in me to do something, but I didn't know what to do.

"God help me. God help me," I whispered. "I..."

I didn't know what to say, and so for a few minutes I sat with Allison's body, alone in silence. In my mind, a picture formed. Allison was walking down a row in a field of wheat that was crowded with people and angelic beings on either side. They were all applauding and cheering like spectators cheering an athlete that was nearly finished with a race. It was a spectacle of lights and joyful cheers. Allison's hair was long and her figure slim once again. She moved slowly at first, as if weak, but picked up momentum as she neared the only person standing before her. It was a man wearing a white robe. A young girl stepped out from behind him, who I immediately knew was our daughter, Eliana. Allison picked up speed and nearly fell into an embrace with the man, who was Jesus. She then wrapped her arms around her daughter, whom she had never met until that moment. Allison showered Eliana with kisses and then the three began to dance together. The crowd erupted into joyful laughter and cheers, as if Allison had won a great victory. The scene radiated jubilance.

I suddenly snapped out of the vision and left the bright field filled with laughter and returned to the dark hospital room, where only silence dwelled. The image could've been a vision, or my own imagination. I had no idea how to distinguish between the two in that moment; however, that didn't change the fact that I knew where Allison now resided.

I whispered, "Now you're seeing what no eye has seen. You're seeing what no ear has heard. You're experiencing what I can only imagine." Tears began to pour down my face. "I promise I'll raise Judah to know Jesus and to know how much you love him. I'll talk to him about you every day. Give our daughter a hug and kiss for me. I'll see you both one day, but not for a long time. I love you so much, Allison. I love you so much."

I wasn't sure what else to say. Since Allison had been hospitalized, we had never once had a conversation about what we wanted to say or what we expected of one another if she would die. We didn't deliberately ignore the topic, but that was how strongly we had believed she would live. At first, I thought to myself what a foolish mistake that had been, and I wondered what I would say to her given the opportunity. Then I realized that Allison and I had known each other so well and so fully that I knew exactly what she would say to me and I to her.

I smiled and raised my hand. My index fixer pointed straight up, and the rest of my fingers tucked into my palm. I bent my index finger down and up twice quickly.

Finally, I stood up and made my way towards the door. I stopped and looked back at Allison's body once more before leaving. "This is not the end," I said. I made our gesture to Allison once more and then left the room for the last time.

In the hallway, my parents and sister waited. They all held boxes that contained Allison's belongings and the many photos and decorations that were once in her room. I looked over all of them and one by one they embraced me. We said nothing as we left the cardiology department.

The next morning family and friends gathered to mourn together. The hospital had provided a room for us and I wept almost uncontrollably when all the men from my Bible study group suddenly walked through the door. They wanted to be there for their brother who had lost his wife. They left their jobs and their families and traveled a great distance to be present for me in my hour of need. I wanted to leave Stanford so badly, but Judah was still hospitalized. Despite the anguish of the situation, I had to remain where he was. Some friends encouraged me to get out of town and take a day trip somewhere, but I refused to leave Judah. His presence nourished and comforted me better than anything else.

I sat in the PICN with Judah in my arms and my sister across from me. I noticed all the families present. Several pairs of parents held, fed, or kissed their babies together. I watched and envied the moms and dads that could be in one another's company. Then I saw something that made me gasp. Across from me was a child that was getting ready to be discharged. The parents were beaming with excitement that they were finally getting to take their baby home. A nurse spoke Spanish to the parents, and I realized the mother was the woman Allison had boldly reassured weeks before in the NICU whose baby boy wasn't expected to live. Not only was that boy alive and seemingly healthy, but he was going home that very day.

"You were right," I whispered.

I was overwhelmed with conflicting feelings of happiness and jealousy. Why was Allison right about all the prophetic things she said to people, even strangers, and yet wrong about herself?

The realization that I was not just a widower but now a single dad had begun to set in. Where was I going to live? What was I going to do for work? How was I going to be a good father and a provider?

I cried and looked up from Judah to Kelly. "How am I going to do this?" I asked my sister.

Kelly knew exactly what I meant and said very matter-of-factly, "With the same grace and excellence Allison would have."

When I finally left the hospital to return to my room, despair struck me like a knife. I couldn't even stand. The thought of my life without Allison seemed too much to bear. Allison wasn't just my wife, she had been my companion in just about everything. We worked together, we shared hobbies, we traveled, we experienced and shared nearly every aspect of our lives. How could I possibly live without her?

I fell to my knees in front of the large, shallow pool and

water fountains in the hospital's main entrance. Moans and cries erupted from my lungs. The skies were filled with dark clouds, and a violent wind tossed leaves and thin branches everywhere around me. It was the first time I had experienced a storm at Stanford. Thunder roared in the distance. It felt as if the planet itself was mourning with me. I wanted to desperately leave the pain and embrace anything that would free me of it...even death. Thoughts of suicide filled my mind.

Suddenly, I heard my father's voice and felt his hand on my shoulder. "Get up, son." I looked up and could see concern and tears on my dad's face. "I know you're hurting right now, but you have a son that needs you and you will always be there for him no matter how bad you're hurting. Do you understand me?"

Before I could respond, my father lifted me to my feet. It was as if he had read my mind and pulled me back from the edge. My fantasy of escape transitioned to thoughts of my son. It wasn't a sense of obligation and duty that steadied me. It was love. I loved my son so much and the thought of leaving him filled me with dread. One day, I would be reunited with Allison again. That was not even a choice for me to make. Death is a part of life; however, I could choose to be strong and present for Judah for as long as possible. He only had one parent in the world, and I needed to love him twice as much now. In that moment, it wasn't a difficult choice to make.

My father joined me in my apartment, where I opened Allison's journal and thumbed through the pages. I skipped ahead to Allison's very last entry which had no date and was barely legible. It said, "*The Lord is my shepherd. Sheep are in many ways the dumbest of all animals. Sheep are completely dependent. Sheep need a shepherd to lead them. Sheep are helpless just like us in so many ways. They have to be led by a good shepherd and God is the great Shepherd. He is calling all of us to stay in the same place until you realize your complete dependency on the Lord. Only then will you find absolute restoration for your soul."*

CHAPTER 33

The next day, I saw an article published about Allison and all we had experienced. It talked about Allison losing her battle with leukemia and the tragedy of her loss. I began to read the online responses from readers below the article and was moved by the comment a family friend, Vanessa, left that said, "Allison didn't lose her battle with leukemia. She won the battle of bringing her little lion into the world to fight, pray and carry on his Mama's legacy and witness. She won the battle of showing this fear-driven world what it looks like to stare death in the face and ask, 'Where is thy sting?' And she won the ultimate prize when she knocked on Heaven's door, leukemia free and heard the words, 'Well Done' from her Jesus."

Vanessa had given Allison the gift of the beloved magnet that said, "Be still and know that I am God." The two ladies had never met in person, but Vanessa was a loud champion and vocal supporter for Allison and Judah.

In the PICN, nurse Melissa embraced me and said how sorry she was. Melissa only knew Allison from the times she took Judah to see her in the ICU and cardiology, but I couldn't help thinking that, given the opportunity, the two of them would've been great friends. Melissa knew I had no intention of leaving the campus while Judah was still in the PICN. He was at thirty-seven weeks gestationally and had to stop having desats before being discharged, in addition to completing other tests and exams. It could be another seven to fourteen days before that happened.

Melissa encouraged me to visit Stanford's Memorial

Church nearby. I had no idea that a church was on the same campus as this massive hospital, research center, and university. In my travels, I had had the opportunity to visit Europe and see the epic cathedrals there. That couldn't prepare me for seeing Stanford's Memorial Church for the first time. It rivaled them all. Even the campus surrounding the main building was a work of art.

A massive courtyard with thousands of hand laid tiles covered the ground and covered walkways with pillars led to the church from several different directions. The upper half of the front of the church was decorated with a colorful mosaic that formed the image of Jesus ministering to a crowd. I had never seen such a massive and intricate piece of art in my life. The mosaic alone must have taken many years to piece together. Incredible stonework and carvings decorated the rest of the front. A sign near the main entrance read: "Memorial Church erected by Jane Lathrop Stanford to the Glory of God and in Loving Memory of Her Husband Leland Stanford."

"Wow..." I said, astonished.

I entered through a large bronze door and discovered the church was even more massive on the inside than it seemed on the outside. The interior was dimly lit, but glowed from the many stained-glass windows and mosaics that depicted a vast number of Biblical stories. More carvings adorned the interior, along with several quotations that were carved into the walls. It was unlike any church I had ever visited. It was as much a work of art as it was a place of worship. One of the quotes near the steps of the altar read, "It is by suffering that God has most nearly approached to man; it is by suffering that man draws most nearly to God."

I saw a stained-glass window depicting Jesus raising Jairus's daughter to life. It was a strange experience to see an image of the account that my mother had read out loud just days before, as Allison was dying.

One quote held my attention longer than the others. It read, "Events are messengers of either Divine goodness or justice. Each has a mission to fulfill and as it comes from God, accomplish it in peace. And, in sending them, the good Father also sends means by which they may be endured, - perhaps averted. Remedies in sickness. Love in trouble. Comfort in weakness. Renewed hope in disappointment. Tears in Sorrow. Smiles to follow tears." The quote made me sad and hopeful at the same time.

I pulled out my phone to take several photos and began to research the history of the building. I was amazed to discover the entire University of Stanford was established as the result of the death of Jane and Leland Stanford's young son. The church itself was erected in response to Leland's death. Out of everything Jane could have done following the death of the last member of her immediate family, she decided to commission the building of a church. Further, I thought it was interesting that the church's dedication sign reads first, "to the Glory of God." Jane, I would discover, had her fair share of tragedies and yet she used her suffering to bring hope to others.

I was inspired by her choices and her determination. Then a thought occurred to me...Should I finish Allison's book myself?

I received a text message from Aileen, one of Allison's favorite nurses in hematology. She asked me to come to see her when I had the opportunity. After finishing my time at the church, I returned to the hematology department for the first time since Allison died. When I arrived, several nurses embraced me, saying how sorry they were and what a wonderful person Allison had been. They showed me a closet filled with gifts for Allison and Judah that were intended to be given during the baby shower the nurses had planned for her.

Aileen approached me and held out her hand. She was holding something long and thin. "When Allison went to the ICU, this got left behind in her old room," she said as she revealed the magnet with the beach design of aquamarine colors and patches of sand and the scripture, "Be still and know that I am God, Psalms 46:10." It was the gift from Vanessa.

Aileen placed the magnet in my hand. "I'm sorry I didn't give it to you earlier," she said. "I think you are supposed to have it now, though."

I sighed. "It's definitely fitting for this moment," I said. "Thank you."

"I'm so sorry, Joshua," Aileen said, embracing me again.

As I left hematology and slowly made my way down the hallways that Allison and I had walked together hundreds of times, my phone chimed.

Allison's best friend, Deborah, messaged me, "Dear Josh. It is with a very heavy heart that I receive the news of Allie's passing. I am forever changed by her presence in my life. I have a burning in my heart to share with you a part of a conversation I had with her the last time I saw her. Allison told me she could not have made it through one minute of this journey without you. She saw and felt your love and devotion to her. She saw your sacrifices on her behalf. She said she never knew she could be loved that much. You are her hero, Josh. She told me so! Know I continue to lift you and Judah in prayer. My love to you all."

I thought of the last few weeks and the condition Allison was in. How there were times I wiped her bottom and cleaned her vomit. It wasn't uncommon to wipe up messes while she was in the ICU or cardiology. Never once was the situation awkward or made me love Allison any less. I never felt like it was my duty to care for her...I cared for Allison because I loved her. In that moment, I longed even for those moments of caring for her to return. I just wanted Allison back.

On September 29, 2015, exactly two weeks after Allison died, Judah finished his final exam and passed his last test. He had gone the required duration of time with no desats in order to be discharged. It was the most bittersweet day of my life. After one hundred seven days, Judah and I were finally leaving Stanford.

Tears of happiness and sorrow flowed down my face as I carried Judah in his car seat down the main hallway of the hospital, with Melissa at my side. My father had pulled his truck up to the loading zone and was waiting for us at the main entrance. As Melissa and I approached the exit, the glass doors slid open automatically. I had passed through them so many times, but this time was different. Allison and I had envisioned, dreamed, and prayed for this moment, but it was all wrong. Judah was supposed to be in Allison's arms and not mine.

Melissa, Judah, and I approached my father's truck. As I opened the back door, Melissa went over some last minute details of life with Judah outside of the hospital, what to expect and how best to care for him. We buckled and secured Judah's car seat into the truck.

I turned to Melissa to say goodbye, but instead I started to cry.

"I'm sorry," Melissa said. "I know this sucks. I'm praying for you guys."

"Thank you for everything," I said.

We embraced and I entered the vehicle next to Judah and shut the door. My dad and I began weeping, while Judah slept soundly.

"Take us home, dad," I said through my tears.

We drove away from Stanford Hospital. For three months, Allison relentlessly fought for that very moment. Every single discomfort, needle, test, scan, infection, fever, sleepless night, treatment, drug, line, tube, pain, round of chemotherapy and even her own life brought about her victory. Allison indeed didn't lose anything, she won. Her goal, first and foremost, was to save the life of her son, and there he sat next to me. Judah was alive because of her and leaving the hospital because Allison had surrendered all. Her love and spirit had seen him through disease and the threat of death and would continue to live on in him. I promised myself and Allison that even though I would ache for her every day of my life, I would tell Judah of the depth of her love for him, and I would raise Judah to know the source of her strength, grace and endless hope, Jesus Christ. In some ways, the journey of healing was complete and, in some ways, it continued. Because of Allison's love and sacrifice, the journey home was beginning.

Part 3

RIDICULOUS HOPE

CHAPTER 34

About halfway to my parent's home, my father pulled over in a fast-food restaurant parking lot so I could change a crying Judah. I lowered the tailgate of the truck and laid Judah down on it instead of taking him inside. Even though Judah had been discharged, he was still in a fairly fragile physical state. Since Allison's own immune system was radically compromised from her disease and treatment, she didn't pass along adequate antibodies to Judah. This made him more vulnerable to viruses and bacteria. Even a cold could be potentially lethal while he built up his immune system over time. With flu season just getting started, it was safer to change him outside than in a public restroom.

My dad left the two of us to get some food and use the bathroom. After I changed Judah, he began to cry again.

"What's wrong buddy? Are you hungry?"

I realized that Judah was definitely due for a bottle, so I prepared some formula and began feeding him. Suddenly, an eerie feeling came upon me. I scanned the parking lot, but we were alone. Then it dawned on me...for the first time in Judah's life, I was alone with him. Every moment of Judah's life, whether in the surgery room, the NICU, PICN or one of Allison's rooms, we always had nurses or doctors accompanying us. This was essentially the first time Judah had ever been alone with just one other human being.

I drew my son close to me as he drank his bottle.

"It's me and you, Judah. I wish mommy could be here too, but it's just you and me," I said.

The only sounds I could hear were of Judah sucking on the bottle. No more beeps from medical monitors or cries from surrounding infants or chatter from parents and staff reached us. It was just the sound of the two of us.

"This isn't too bad," I whispered to him.

Later, as my dad pulled into his driveway, I asked him to give me a minute. My dog Lilo ran out of the house to greet me. I hadn't seen her since we had left for Stanford. I lifted Judah's car seat out of the truck and placed it onto the ground in front of Lilo. The chocolate lab sniffed Judah and cocked her head at him curiously.

"You're his dog now, too, Lilo. Keep an eye on him for me," I said.

I petted Lilo lovingly and cried as her head turned and she searched the truck as if to look for Allison. "Mommy's not coming back, girl," I said. "She wanted to see you again so badly. She wanted to be here. I'm sorry she's not." Lilo walked alongside me as we entered my parent's home.

My parents had given Allison and I their spare bedroom before we went to Stanford and it had now been made up for me and Judah. With Judah's immune system in a weakened state, there was no telling when it would be safe for him to travel and going back to New Zealand wasn't realistic without Allison. For the foreseeable future, the spare bedroom in my parent's house would be our home.

For a long time, I just paced around the house and held Judah to my chest. I was a storm of thoughts and feelings. The joy of having my first born in my arms as a counterpart to the agony of losing my spouse had made me numb. I had so many things to do and so many questions about the future. Allison's memorial service needed to be planned and I needed to cancel everything that was still active under her name. While it wasn't an immediate concern, I couldn't help wondering what I was going to do for employment and where Judah and I would eventually live. Every single plan I had for our future was over.

For as long as we lived with my parents, we wouldn't have any financial burdens. All of our medical bills would be paid for by the financial aid program. In addition, the money our community had raised for us was in a savings account. Eventually I could use it to start over. I wondered if I should reopen my business. Did I even want to do that without Allison? I forced myself to focus on the present. For now, my sole job and responsibility was to take care of the child in my arms.

I never envisioned being a single father. It was quite a contrast from living with Allison to now be sharing a home with my parents, my infant son and three dogs. We assembled an infant's bed that was elevated enough so that Judah was right beside me when I slept. Our room was very cramped. Between my bed, the crib, a dresser, and a rocking chair there was barely any room to maneuver. My parents and I decorated with many of the same things Allison had put up in her hospital room. Photos of us were everywhere, as well as Allison's artwork. The room was filled with color and a vibrancy I appreciated.

Above the dresser, I hung Paula's picture of Allison holding a smiling baby Judah, with my arms around them both. We all looked healthy and happy. The image that was meant to give hope, and indeed had, now left me with mixed feelings, but I kept it on the wall.

I recalled the word we'd heard at City Impact Church

that, for some members of the congregation, 2015 was going to be the year of the whirlwind. Within a timeframe of just eight months, we had found out Allison was pregnant, closed our business, sold all of our belongings, moved to New Zealand, Allison was diagnosed with leukemia, we returned to the United States, Allison was admitted to Stanford, Judah was born, Allison died, and Judah and I now lived with my parents. Calling it a whirlwind was the understatement of the century.

As I opened several packages from supporters, friends, and family, I came across one that contained an art print of a scroll and a quill. Written on the scroll was the word "Healing", but the glass frame had been completely destroyed during shipping. Broken glass filled the package and had made deep scratches on the print in several places.

"Healing..." I read the word aloud. I shook my head and began to cry. "No more than a broken promise."

I threw the image and the broken frame in the trash.

Loneliness and heartache, accompanied by sleepless nights, consumed me during the days leading up to Allison's memorial service. I poured myself into editing several videos, slide shows and writing a speech. I read the speech aloud to myself over and over until I was able to do it without crying. Part of me craved help in the planning process, but, in my desire to ensure Allison had the best, I decided to do most of it on my own.

On October 17, a congregation of nearly one thousand came together to remember Allison's life. I had edited several videos that included excerpts from our "Journey of Healing" videos. It was a strange but profound sight seeing and hearing Allison speak at her own memorial service. As another slideshow and video I'd created containing clips of Allison dancing on the stage at church played, a fellow dancer and friend of Allison's, danced along. She danced on the stage while Allison danced on the video screen above her. Then, a multitude of voices filled the church as we sang several of Allison's favorite worship songs together. As our worship concluded, I stepped onto the stage.

"Good morning." I began my speech by expressing my gratitude, "your generosity and encouragement is what gave us so much strength during this fight...Thank you for continually uplifting my wife when she needed it most. On February 15, 2005..." I continued to share about Allison, how we met, her life, her courage, her faith, and the legacy of love she left behind in Judah. As I spoke, it dawned on me for the first time that Allison's name could be broken down into three separate words: "All," "I" and "Son." It was as if even her name indicated that she would give everything for her beloved son.

It was hard for my mind not to wander as I read my speech. I was standing on the same stage Allison and I had been married on. The same stage Allison had danced and worshiped God on many times in front of the congregation. I had filmed interviews, spoken to the congregation, both of us had performed in various church plays, musicals, and skits in the very place I was standing. Now it had also become the place from which I shared Allison's eulogy.

"Allison, you finished the race so well, my love," I started my conclusion. "Allison didn't lose her battle with leukemia...she remained steadfast and strong in her will; she strove to finish the race, she sought Christ in all things, in the midst of a joyless situation she found joy, and she never yielded to despair. Instead, she surrendered to hope. She WON the battle of bringing her little lion into the world...In that, I ask you now to rise as we celebrate Allison's life by welcoming her victory to the stage. Please welcome our son, Judah Aslan Cordero."

Judah was brought up to the stage and I held him while together, as a faith-filled community, we prayed for Judah and his future.

Later that evening, at a reception for close friends and family, many spoke and shared memories of Allison. Tarry and Lisa had to remain in New Zealand and were unable to attend the service, however, Tarry sent a message that he asked me to read at the reception, and not before. I shared that little detail with everyone because I had no idea what to expect. I cried as I read the words Tarry had written for me and everyone else to hear:

> "To our dear friend Josh, I once said to you that it was not about the destination, it was all about the journey. Wow, who would have ever imagined your journey would have taken you where it has. It is with broken hearts that we join with you today in remembering your gorgeous Allison. This quiet, understated lady has made an everlasting impact on our lives. Her example of selflessness, sacrifice and unfaltering trust in God continues to inspire us to no end. She died how she lived, completely and totally surrendered to her Lord and Savior. We can only hope to live our lives in the same manner. Josh, we cannot begin to imagine what life without Allison is like for you, but we continue to pray grace, grace, grace; for His grace is sufficient. Baby

Judah. Your parents named you Judah for good reason. The very fact that you are alive today is a testament to the goodness and graciousness of God, for which we give Him great praise. Little man, know this, your mother was the bravest person we have ever met. She loved you more than life itself and willingly gave everything for you. There is no greater love than this. Josh, the fact remains, your journey continues. We know that this is not the end of the movie, but just the end of that heartbreaking scene where all seems lost and leaves the audience wondering – 'what will the hero do now?' You are that hero Josh, and we are amazed at your fortitude and strength to keep on keeping on. There are of course many more adventures yet to be seen and we will continue to watch with much anticipation..."

The next two days I busied myself with filling out paperwork and cancelling accounts for Allison, like her cell phone plan, health insurance and subscriptions. I had just finished the last of my errands when my dad called.

"Judah won't wake up from his nap," he said anxiously.

CHAPTER 35

"What?" I asked, dumbfounded.

"Is he breathing?" I asked.

"Well, yes, of course, but he won't stay awake," my dad answered.

Judah was in an unusually deep sleep and they were having trouble waking him. We had just seen a pediatrician and were planning a series of checkups, tests, and exams for Judah to ensure that he didn't have any challenges or abnormalities in his development. Other than his immune system still recuperating, he had been pronounced completely healthy during his last checkup.

"Maybe he's just really tired."

"Son, this isn't normal. Get back over here now."

"I'm sure he's fine."

"You need to see him for yourself."

My dad and I went back and forth. I became irritated and didn't take him seriously. I even went as far as to accuse him of being a fear monger. I reluctantly returned to my parents' home; certain they were overreacting.

Once home, I was able to wake Judah up, but he couldn't keep his eyes open. He didn't cry and barely moved in response to my waking him. Judah should not only have been awake, but he should've been crying. His breathing seemed fine, but dad was right. Something was wrong.

My parents and I took Judah to the pediatrician right away, where we explained what was happening. Other than seeming overly fatigued, Judah didn't have any other symptoms. He had no fever and, despite not being his usual animated self, he stayed awake enough to begin drinking from a bottle while my parents explained what had happened.

My father elaborated that Judah had been sleeping in a rocker and made an odd sound. My dad approached him and noticed that, while Judah's color was fine, he didn't seem to be breathing. In response, my father gently touched him, and Judah suddenly inhaled loudly and deeply. Did Judah almost die in his sleep? I continued to feed Judah as the pediatrician listened intently to my parents.

Judah suddenly lowered his head and a little bit of formula spilled from his mouth. He looked up at me and seemed to smile. Then, his head dropped down to his chest and his face turned purple.

"He's not breathing!" I screamed.

I rubbed Judah's body vigorously, but he still wouldn't take a breath. I didn't even know how to perform CPR on an infant, so I laid Judah on the exam table while the pediatrician opened the door to the room and shouted, "Call 911!"

She then dashed towards Judah and began CPR. My parents started praying urgently. A nurse came in and fumbled with an oxygen tank and mask that didn't seem to work properly. Judah suddenly took a breath and his color slowly started to come back, but he wasn't breathing consistently.

"God, if he dies, then everything Allison sacrificed was for nothing," I couldn't help thinking.

I talked to Judah and rubbed his limbs and chest while praying. After a few agonizing minutes, EMTs burst into the room. They attached all-too-familiar looking cables and monitors to Judah as he was placed on a gurney and rolled out of the exam room. I walked beside Judah, held his hand, and continued to talk to him. As we passed through the lobby, I glanced up and saw a room full of waiting parents and children. Every mom and dad seemed to be holding their children extra close to them.

I rode in an ambulance with Judah to the ER. He was continuously stimulated and given oxygen. Without the stimulation and support, he would quickly stop breathing again. Flight paramedics arrived a short time later and prepared to fly Judah to the nearest children's hospital, fifty miles away. They wouldn't let me fly with Judah, and I had to restrain my anger and protests.

As we drove to the hospital in Madera, I was terrified that Judah could be dying, and I wasn't able to be there with him. I was in hell. Allison had died just a month before, and now, just two days after her memorial service, this new nightmare had befallen us.

I sprinted through the large, open lobby of the children's hospital and towards the nearest elevator. The hospital was difficult to navigate in the midst of my panic, but I eventually found my way to the emergency department and shouted, "I'm Judah's dad! Where's Judah Cordero?"

A few moments later, I found Judah's exam room, where a man and woman in medical gowns were working on him. Judah was crying and thrashing his limbs. As I stepped into the room, they put up their hands for me to stop and insisted I put on a medical gown and mask for Judah's safety. After I covered myself, I approached Judah, who had now stabilized. He had a nasal cannula attached to his face. Seeing him in a hospital room once again, rigged up with tubes, cables and monitors left me shaky and unable to breathe or think clearly.

It had only been a few weeks since he had been discharged from Stanford and we were back in another hospital. How did this happen? There were no prayers I could force myself to whisper. No curses I was capable of muttering or even tears I could shed. I had nothing left in me.

I leaned over Judah's bed and gently slid the tip of my finger into his hand. He firmly closed and gripped around it.

I shuddered and said, "Keep fighting, Judah."

For ten days, Judah remained in the hospital. He had been diagnosed with parainfluenza, a respiratory virus. The medical team met with me several times to go over his and Allison's medical history. They explained to me just how sensitive Judah was to infections, especially during the flu season, because of his prematurity and Allison's inability to pass on adequate antibodies to him.

For the sake of Judah's survival, it was suggested that anyone who was living with Judah get their flu shots as well as several other immunizations and immunity boosting shots. No one who was, or recently had been, sick or lived in the same household of someone who was sick should be allowed to enter our home. If we were to return from a store or a trip to town, we should first shower, put on fresh clothes and only then hold Judah. Cold, flu and respiratory viruses could easily be on our clothes and then passed to Judah.

I had to restrain myself from breaking down when I realized the extent of Judah's fragility. While he had been kept safely away from everyone at Allison's memorial service, it dawned on me that hundreds and hundreds of people hugged me during the event. When it finished, the first thing I had done was go into a private room with Judah and hold him close to me. I held him against the same suit jacket that so many others had rubbed against as they embraced me to offer their condolences.

"Oh God..." I groaned.

In all likelihood, I was the one who had exposed my son to the virus that nearly killed him, simply by having him at Allison's memorial service. Not only that, but my father had saved Judah's life by trying to stimulate him when Judah had held his breath, and also by ignoring my protests and insisting that we take him to the pediatrician. I was overridden with guilt.

On the drive home from the hospital, I shook my head in anguish. Allison's death was terrible enough. I had hoped to have the love and company of friends and family during my time of mourning. I longed for some semblance of normalcy, and that included having people over to love on my infant son! Even that was denied to me.

"You keep finding ways to steal my joy, don't you," I muttered to God. "Not only mine, but Judah's too. He can't even have people over to hold him. You let his mother die and now you've driven us into isolation. What good are you?"

CHAPTER 36

On November 2, a beautiful ocean view was before me as I watched the sun go down, from the balcony of a hotel room that Allison and I had frequented when we visited the beach. I wondered how many sunsets Allison and I had watched from this hotel over the years. On an end table next to me sat the urn that contained Allison's remains. A few years before, we had discussed whether we would want to be buried or cremated.

"Spread my ashes at a place that is precious to us. Someplace beautiful with lots of happy memories. That's what I'd want you to think of anyway, the good times and happy memories." Allison had once told me.

"Does any place come to mind?" I had asked her.

"I don't care. I'll be dead," Allison had said, laughing. "This is for you, not me! And for the record, you're not dying before me," she had said.

"What?" I exclaimed.

"I don't want a life without us together. That's just...not for me. Nope. Sorry," Allison had said, half joking, but half serious as well.

I had thought for a few moments and named a coast that was very dear to us.

"That sounds perfect," Allison had said.

"It is perfect," I said now, as I stood barefoot on wet sand and looked out across the coastline. The next day would've been our eight-year anniversary, and instead of celebrating our lives together, I would be celebrating the memory of it. I planned to spend part of the day revisiting memorable locations in town and eventually spread Allison's ashes in the same place where we had experienced so many happy moments.

It was surprisingly hard to sleep that night. For the first time since I had moved in with my parents, I had a room to myself. With all that had happened with Judah I didn't want to risk exposing him to anything, so my father had volunteered to stay home with him. Without him next to me, I thought I would experience a peaceful night of sleep for a change, but I kept thinking about him and wondering how he was doing. I was lonely without him.

The next morning, I drove to the resort where Allison and I had spent our honeymoon. We had rarely stayed there since then because it was too expensive for us, but we would sometimes visit the diner or restaurant to eat. I entered the diner to have breakfast and, sure enough, our table was available: a small two-seater table beside a large circular window. Every single time the two of us ate breakfast there, we'd be seated at the same table. Allison thought it was cute.

I didn't feel comfortable leaving Allison's urn inside my truck, so I placed it on the seat across from me. It felt awkward, and it was an unpleasant feeling to have my wife's remains in the same seat she had occupied so many times. I stood my phone up against the napkin holder on the table and pulled up a picture of Allison sitting in the very chair in front of me from a previous anniversary. She was holding up a cup of coffee and smiling.

After ordering breakfast, I sat and remembered the past and pondered the future. We had taken pleasure in the simplest things because we shared them with each other. Now, I had to redefine what the little things meant to me. Would the same hobbies and activities still be appealing now that Allison was no longer here to share them with me? The thought of future anniversaries, birthdays and holidays without Allison just seemed so...empty. Without her, the vibrancy of those events was absent. I began to get sick to my stomach, but forced myself to think about what Allison would want me to do. It didn't take long for me to dwell on what an extraordinarily generous person she was. If these events were to still be meaningful and full of joy, then they needed to be accompanied by Allison's spirit, if not her physical presence. I thought of how she'd hand out coffee gift cards to fellow parents and patients at Stanford. There was no better way to celebrate than to continue her spirit of generosity and giving.

My gaze lifted from the photo of Allison and I scanned the room to look at the other patrons. An elderly couple caught my eye. I called over my waitress and said I wanted to anonymously treat the couple to their meal. Just as my food arrived, the couple finished theirs. I watched as the waitress told them that their bill had been taken care of. The woman seemed literally startled! While I couldn't hear their words, it was obvious they were trying to probe the waitress for the identity of their benefactor. They looked around the room for any signs of who it could be. Ironically, they never even looked at me!

When she returned, the waitress shared that the couple was so grateful and said they had never experienced anything like that in their lives. I smiled. Allison believed that, as Christians, our daily actions are our loudest ministry. Those actions didn't have to be anything overtly Christian. They just had to be selfless, authentic, and generous. That was how she lived and that was how I was going to survive the events and milestones that lay ahead: by thinking about others.

I finished my meal and sipped at the last of my coffee. It felt cheesy, but I stared at the photo of Allison beaming with her own cup of coffee. I couldn't help holding up my mug and saying, "Happy anniversary, Allie. I'm...." My voice caught in my throat and I had to compose myself so I wouldn't cry. "I'm really going to miss all the coffees."

Leaving the restaurant, I headed to our favorite beach to meet up with a small group of family members. At this beach, Allison and I had our first kiss and took many long walks, often with a hot cup of coffee. Allison had loved taking photos around this whole area. Many rocks and towering boulders are scattered across the coastline and out into the water. It made for a beautiful setting. After we prayed, I made my way into the water with the urn full of Allison's remains in my hands. It was hard to comprehend that this urn held all that remained of the physical part of my beloved. I said nothing but wept as I poured the ashes into the waves and water.

Allison had treasured several beautiful spots within close proximity, so I walked to each one and poured a portion of her ashes out at all of them. When only a little remained, I submerged the urn and let the tide take the rest out. Just like that, it was finished. The memorial service was over, Judah and I were settled into my parents' home, all of the tedious paperwork had been finished, and now Allison's ashes had been dispersed. There were no more plans, just a sea of questions and an ocean of thoughts and memories.

I stood overlooking the rocks and the waves and whispered, "Happy anniversary, Allison. You were the greatest honor, pleasure and adventure of my life." I held up my index finger and bent it down and up twice.

CHAPTER 37

The days and nights became a blur of monotonous routines filled with loneliness, sleepless nights, mourning, and fear that Judah could catch another virus at any moment and perish. I was in survival mode. I rarely left the house, and we hardly had any guests. Just about everyone we knew was sick, or someone in their household was sick, that winter. Still, in the midst of it all, Judah filled my heart with an undeniable happiness when I needed it most.

The most comforting part of my day was simply holding his bare skin against mine as I listened to him breathe. More often than not, he'd be in my arms or lying flat on my chest. My parents both worked full-time, so I cared for Judah on my own during the day. Our only outings were short drives through town, and coffee and food at a drive through.

Most nights I cried myself to sleep, thinking of Allison and longing for her to be beside me. I wanted to wake up and see her holding Judah. I wanted us to fight over how best to care for him and go on long walks together with our son. I longed for a single memory of us outside of the hospital. I recounted the same questions over and over again to my parents about Allison. Why didn't God save her? What was the point of us moving to New Zealand? Why did we experience some miracles and not others?

Tarry moved forward with production of City Impact Church's first feature film as the writer and director. It was called "Broken." We did not communicate very much. I was extraordinarily jealous of his endeavors and accomplishments and in the end, I think he thought including me would be too painful.

Depression set in and, after several months, my parents insisted I see a grief counselor. When I sat with the man, he was initially speechless at my story.

"Josh," he said. "I know you technically can't help it, but you're doing the two worst things you could possibly do during the death of a spouse. You're not sleeping, and you've isolated yourself."

Like many people do during therapy sessions, I found myself doing most of the talking, which ended up being helpful. As I recounted the details of the journey Allison and I had been on, I realized it wasn't just Allison that I was mourning, but also the life I thought I'd have. Allison and I had moved to another country with the expectation we would make a movie, helm TV shows, and have our first child in a beautiful new country. It had been scary, but also so exciting! God seemed to open all the right doors to make incredible things happen because we had stepped out in faith. Our dreams and desires had come to fruition all at once and then everything fell out from under us.

I shook my head as I spoke to my counselor, "Every single plan I had for our lives is over now..." I froze suddenly.

"Are you alright, Josh?" the counselor asked.

"Yeah... give me just a minute." I said, and then began to think out loud, sharing about the encounter Allison and I had at St. Anthony's Retreat on New Year's Eve.

"Allison and I had been so desperate to know what God had in store for us that next year. In response, God told us the same word, 'Surrender.' When we asked him what we were supposed to surrender, He told me, 'Surrender your plans for the future.'"

In truth, I had very much thought of that answer as figurative and that He was telling me to trust Him; that He had bigger plans for me than I did for myself. Now, with Allison gone, the opportunities in New Zealand gone and living as a full-time single parent, I couldn't help thinking of how literal that statement was. Every single plan I made for life had been undone. They all included Allison. They included us being healthy and going on adventures. Not this. I didn't plan on any of this. This was not the future I expected, hoped for, or wanted.

"God told Allison to surrender motherhood," I continued. In that moment, I realized the full weight of that statement and began to weep uncontrollably.

When God had first spoken to Allison, we were confused. Years before, He had told us through Bobby Hill that Allison would "bear children," and God had told me we'd have a son and to name him "Judah."We speculated that perhaps we had misunderstood. Maybe God meant she wouldn't get pregnant again and she had to release that desire. Were we supposed to adopt? The more we discussed it, the more convoluted it seemed. Allison wanted to become pregnant more than anything in the world, but she wanted God's will for her life even more. Her desire to give birth to a healthy baby remained, but she released the plan of it ever happening.

Just seven days after Allison surrendered that desire to God, she conceived Judah, but she never got to be with Judah outside of the hospital. She didn't get to breastfeed Judah, change his diaper, care for him, nor would she have the opportunity to raise him. While Allison got to experience the longing of her heart and become a mother, she never got to truly experience motherhood. She had surrendered it.

I knew that nothing in our lives came as a surprise to God and that, combined with my revelation, filled me with anger and made my blood boil. God knew this was going to happen! He had sent us to New Zealand and Allison received the blood test that caught the leukemia in the nick of time. Because we had moved and sold everything we had, we possessed no assets and qualified for financial assistance. God had told Allison to keep our health insurance and since there were no commitments or work obligations of any kind, I was able to stay with Allison and Judah at all times during their horrible battles. It was so obvious that there had been several big things that God had orchestrated that prepared us for Allison's fight.

"If God could do all of that then why didn't He just heal her?" I brokenly said.

The thought of Allison's book filled my mind and the motivation I had to one day finish it vanished. What good could come from our story? How could a story of a God who had directed our every step, only to have it end in Allison's death, bring anyone any semblance of hope?

When I finished speaking, the counselor, who was a Spirit-filled Christian, prayed for me. I said nothing and just cried as he prayed, but my trust in God's love, His will, and His plans had vanished.

After a few minutes, the counselor paused and said, "Joshua I really believe God wants to tell you...and this is very hard for me to say, because even to me it seems cruel...but God wants to tell you the things that transpired...they ended the way they did because of how much you two trusted Him. They ended the way they did because of your decision to surrender all to Him. Does that make sense?"

Events spanning years began to connect in my mind as the past and present collided once more. I remembered what Bobby Hill told Allison and I six years before in 2009 that, "There shall be unexpected developments in your life, and it shall even cause you to shake to the very core. You will say, 'My God, why is this happening? Why are we in this situation? Why do we have to go through this change?' The Lord says, 'Never question the potter's intention because my hands are around you. And I am shaping you and yes, I will re-shape and break and re-make you several times so that I may have just the right vessels. For I have taken you at your word when you said, "We Surrender."'"

Salvation was one thing. It was another thing entirely to release your greatest desires and the longing to control your own life. Allison and I loved God and trusted Him enough to do just that. We had sincerely laid down everything we were and everything we wanted to be and declared, "Use us as You see fit." Allison and I surrendered our jobs, our security, our home, our plans, our finances, our hopes, our dreams, and our lives. God listened and took us at our word.

I shuddered and, for a moment, I thought I was going to pass out.

That prophetic word revolved around a decision we wouldn't make until years later in 2014 when we told God, "We surrender" and came to its full fruition for Allison when she died on September 15, 2015.

"God, what are you doing?" I asked. I could not wrap my head around what I had learned. I believed God was a God of love, but was this love? Was this what a Heavenly Father did to His children when they trusted Him?

When we attended the School of Creativity, Shawn Bolz had prophesied that we would be, "...a signpost of favor" and to "...get ready for a harvest of favor and opportunity." Was this favor?

While I longed for company, I found myself hating being around people. Too often my family and I heard that question, "Have things gone back to normal?". I was never sure how to take that question. Normal had perished with Allison. I had to rediscover and redefine what normal was for me. There wasn't a normal to return to. It was such an absurd question.

As the weeks stretched on, I would hear frustrating and sometimes ridiculous phrases over and over again from people like, "Now Allison is Judah's angel," "Everything happens for a reason," "You'll be reunited in Heaven one day," "She's in a better place," "God's ways are bigger than ours," "She's not hurting anymore."

One doctor examined Judah, and after hearing about Allison's death commented, "Now you just need to find this boy a new mommy."

People will never truly understand something until it happens to them. I know the comments were spoken out of love, but I wished most people would have just said nothing at all. I knew my community wanted to help or to say anything that could lessen my pain, but I began to resent their efforts.

One man I barely knew approached me in a parking lot and said, "Josh, can I just give you a hug?"

I told him it was okay, and he embraced me.

"I am so sorry for what you're going through. I just want to let you know that my family is praying for you and if there's anything you guys ever need just say so. Do you need anything?"

"I'm okay for now. Thank you, though."

It was perfect. No rationalizing. No trying to justify what happened. Just acknowledgment of my pain and expressing care and love. It was a sharp contrast to the man at my church who told me, "Sometimes God takes something away so He can give us something better," or the person who declared Allison perished because we didn't have enough faith God would heal her. For some reason, people kept sharing stories with me of other husbands who lost their wives. I'm not sure how they thought it would help.

People often sent me songs they found uplifting. Most of the time I never listened to them. I didn't know what I wanted from people. I hated them when they didn't reach out to me and I hated them when they did.

Reading comments from my occasional social media posts was the closest thing to consistent human interaction I had that didn't irritate me. Despite all my frustrations, I appreciated all the prayers. Many strangers messaged me about how Allison's story had impacted their lives. Some people even shared that they, or someone they knew and loved, came to Christ, or started going to church as a result of hearing Allison's story. Something about her journey of selflessness, love and sacrifice resonated with people.

I had mixed feelings. In one moment, I'd be happy Allison's testimony was already touching lives and, in the next,

I'd be filled with anger. The transformation these people experienced came at the cost of Allison's life. Did she have to die for them to have their moment with God? I'd rather have Allison with me and Judah. I loved and raged against my supporters. Every day and night I found myself asking, why all the miracles? Why all the hope? If Allison was going to die anyway, why did she miraculously survive Judah's birth? Why did she have prophetic dreams of having more children? Why did Allison receive all the prophetic words about having twin girls? Prophecy is certainly real. I had seen it, experienced it, and even imparted it, but the situation left me full of doubt and distrust.

One day, I poured out the contents of Allison's three vases and read through all the things she had written during the course of her hospitalization. I read through scores of prayers that were answered and dozens that were not. All the things Allison wanted to do and experience after she was discharged left me weeping on the floor. From grand things like writing a book and traveling around the world to tell of God's goodness, to simply going on a walk with me and Judah; the vase held so many hopes, plans and dreams but, above all, it revealed the relentless faith Allison displayed. A faith that was betrayed.

I tried to talk to Tarry who, like many, tried to hypothesize and rationalize. He wondered if perhaps Allison miscarried twins or maybe I would remarry one day, and that woman would have twins. Perhaps the dreams Allison had of her life continuing outside of the hospital were to simply give her hope. A goal to fight for.

His words angered and frustrated me. Was that hope a

lie?

I imagined a soldier in a fierce battle whose weapon is depleted of all its ammunition. His hope of winning the battle, let alone survive, is waning. If someone handed that soldier a huge stack of magazines and ammo his hope and ferocity to keep fighting would indeed be renewed but, what if he slid one of those fresh magazines into his rifle and pulled the trigger only to realize he was firing blanks? He had been given the hope to keep fighting but not the means to win. What good was that?

For Allison and me, the fires of hope had been lit for us to see but, before we could even feel their warmth, the flames had been extinguished. God had essentially sat on His capable hands and watched Allison die.

One morning, Chad re-sent the message to me that he had shared when Allison was hospitalized. "...I got this picture of a dandelion being blown on by God. I saw the pods being blown off and being replanted all across a barren field..." I remembered how encouraging it had been when we first received it and continued to read each word carefully. "I'm reminded that God never wastes suffering. He redeems all of it for His glory and our blessing...."

Chad continued his message with one new comment. "Thinking about you this morning and I can't help but think of all the potential questions that are going through your mind. I hope I'm not stepping over any boundaries with you, but I really feel like you need to know that you did not misunderstand God when He spoke specific promises to you. I believe they are still there for you to take. I was reminded of Hebrews 11 this morning. It mentions Abraham in part of the chapter, and I thought about the amazing promise God gave him and yet he only experienced part of the promise. The promise extended far past his life. I want to remind you what you heard from God is true and your promise is not dead, but it is far greater than you can ever imagine. God's promise to you extends for generations not just for a single lifetime."

His words were uplifting, but I couldn't help thinking that, as Christians, we'd praise God when a miracle presented itself and, in the absence of one, we'd declare He worked in mysterious ways. It seemed like a cop-out.

Before I knew it, Thanksgiving was upon us, and managed to be an enjoyable day with family. Judah was getting bigger and was the source of joy for all of us. The day after Thanksgiving, on the other hand, was more difficult. It had always been full of tradition for Allison and me in previous years. We'd put up all of our Christmas lights on the house and setup the many decorations inside. Allison liked to buy Christmas ornaments when we visited new places. Many of them held a memory or story that we'd relive while hanging it up on the tree. She loved to blast Christmas albums from her favorite artists, usually Jeremy Camp or Phil Wickham, and sing along while she decorated. We'd typically binge watch the Thanksgiving and Christmas episodes of our favorite shows and go get coffee before taking a long walk in the downtown area. The knowledge that those traditions were no more weighed on me so much that I felt like I couldn't breathe.

That day, my parents remained at home with Judah while I took a drive with no real destination in mind. I drove until I had no idea where I was. The paved road disappeared, and I ended up on a dirt road surrounded by empty fields. Not a single home or building were in sight. I parked my truck and marched out of the vehicle into a dirt field and began screaming. The air filled with my angry protests and the loathing I had for God and the situation I was in. I wanted my wife back. I wanted my son to be healthy. I wanted the life I thought I would have. I fell to my knees in the dirt and cursed God for drawing me so close to Him only to rip my heart out.

"You're not worth it! Everything You do is unfair and corrupt! Prove me wrong! Do something! Say anything! Show me You actually give a damn!"

I waited for a response for several minutes but there was only silence. Tears, dust, and snot covered my face. My sanity felt like a mask that was finally slipping away. Exhaustion, grief, and fear culminated in an explosion of desperation.

Opening the passenger door to my truck, I swiped out all of the items that were on the seat.

"Look! I made a place for her to sit, now bring Allison back!" I shouted. "Even now I know You can! I know it's in Your power to bring her back to life. Her ashes are in the sea and yet I still know You can call her out of the waves! Do a damn miracle! You told me our lives were going to be a story and You told Allison to write a book about us so make a fucking ending that has some semblance of good! That shows You are a good God and not a monster!"

I sobbed and looked at the seat. I truly expected that Allison might appear, but it remained empty. With nothing left, I collapsed to the ground. I heard and felt a dull thud as I hit the side of my truck on the way down. I didn't get up and remained there for a long time with the passenger door still open. No

words, cries, or tears came from me anymore that day. Just
brokenness.

CHAPTER 38

Just about anytime I heard a sermon or worship song, I became angry. The promises and declarations of a loving and faithful God no longer rang true. I knew God existed, but I didn't love or trust Him. I kept trying to connect with Him only to pull back every time. I grew weary of people approaching me at my home church, so my mother insisted I visit the church that Allison and I had occasionally attended, where I could attend more anonymously. We decided to go together.

The Saturday evening service began with worship songs. I stood when the congregation did, but I refused to participate. My eyes searched the auditorium of strangers until I suddenly saw a familiar face. It was the older man, Lawrence, who had always removed an aisle seat to make space for his wife, Carol, and her wheelchair. I had nearly forgotten about our experience with them. Their love for one another was always so evident. I realized that Carol's wheelchair was not where it typically was. Lawrence was by himself. I wondered if she was okay or even still alive, but I had no desire to go ask. I wanted to keep to myself.

I snickered, rolled my eyes, and ground my teeth during many of the pastor's talking points. I wondered how many people had truly walked through a season of darkness and still believed God loved them unconditionally. I had walked through fire with Allison. The flames burned away my hope and faith and extinguished her life entirely! The pastor's next words caused me to get up and storm off into the bathroom. I punched a stall door several times, cried and cursed. I would've

357

gone home, but my mother remained inside.

When the service ended, I walked into the sanctuary and noticed she had gone up front for prayer. I cursed at the fact that I had to wait for her and sat in a chair near the back. As I waited, I noticed Lawrence near the front. He had just finished speaking with someone and glanced in my direction. I pretended not to notice him, but in my peripheral vision I saw him making his way towards me. I cursed again and looked down. I hoped he was heading towards the exit to go home and hadn't actually seen me. There was a good chance he might not even remember who I was.

"Hey, Joshua," Lawrence said.

I mentally cursed several times and feigned surprise as I greeted him.

"How is Allison doing?" Lawrence asked. Suddenly, my irritation and anger slipped into vulnerable sadness. I cried as I told him everything that had happened over the previous few months.

"How are you handling your grief?" Lawrence asked.

"Not very well," I told him bluntly.

Lawrence then began to share about the loss of his wife. Carol had died less than a week after Allison had. For the first time, I got to hear the scope of the physical battle Carol had experienced. Many years before, she had defeated breast cancer, but later developed bone cancer. The strain of her disease and treatment brought on two strokes that left half her body paralyzed. As Lawrence shared about his own grief, he emphasized the need to go deeper with God, how agonizing grief is, and how it's one of the greatest opportunities to draw close to God. He asked about my trust in God. I confessed my mindset, believing God to be a liar, and that I felt He had betrayed us.

Lawrence nodded, "How much time did you spend with Allison on earth?"

"A little over ten years. We were married for seven," I answered.

"Did you experience a lot of love and good times during those years?" Lawrence asked.

"A lot and so many, yes." I answered.

"Then..." he explained, "if you have the audacity to demand answers to the 'whys' of God taking Allison, you have to also demand the 'whys' of Him allowing you to spend ten incredible years with her."

I had never quite thought of it that way and in truth if anyone else had said that, I would've walked away. Instead, I continued to listen.

"Joshua, you need to focus on what God has done instead of what He did not. You can't condemn God for failing to act without acknowledging all the action He did take. Neither can you demand answers to questions without being grateful for the answers you already know. You can't demand an explanation for why Allison was taken without also demanding why she was given to you in the first place. We aren't able to challenge grief without equally challenging grace. If you want God to give you answers about why He allowed her to die you have to be able to listen when He gives you answers about why He allowed her to live for twenty-nine years."

I couldn't respond and instead just cried and listened.

"God does not waste suffering," Lawrence continued, "He uses it to mold us and shape us. After life leaves us entirely broken and, in a state where we are at our most pliable, able to be re-shaped and molded into something grand...that's when God is at His greatest. When the fragments of our souls are so shattered and dispersed across the vastness of suffering, to the point where we don't even know ourselves, when we're just raw material, it is only then that God can truly make us into a new creation. If suffering is a fire that God can use to forge us into the most refined and resilient of spirits, then the greatest opportunity for us to rise is after we've descended lower than we ever thought possible. Anyone can see God in the big things, but it takes real spiritual discipline to see Him in the details of suffering. He only allows the children He trusts the most to walk through the darkest valleys of death. True greatness awaits those who have endured the lowest of seasons and can still say their hope and trust is in Jesus."

He then quoted Romans 5:2-5, "Not only so, but we also glory in our sufferings because we know that suffering produces perseverance; perseverance character; and character, hope. And hope does not put us to shame because God's love has been poured out into our hearts through the Holy Spirit who has been given to us."

I thought of how Allison hoped until the very end and in that moment the vision I had of her walking between a crowd of spectators towards Jesus and Eliana took on a whole new meaning. I knew now that the crowd was cheering for her because of how well she had lived and died with hope and faith in her God.

Lawrence continued, "Tribulation is necessary for the destabilization of oneself. If God's going to build us up in His image, He must first level the unstable house of cards that we once thought was our self-constructed tower of resilience and strength. Your suffering can either make you bitter and hardened or it can make you soft and humble, and deepen you heart to love more fully. What an opportunity you now have, Joshua! Sorrow and grief soak up vast amounts of shallowness, too, let me tell you!"

Lawrence shared one profound thing after another with me. Before long, we were the only two in the whole auditorium. He asked more questions about my journey and listened to all that Allison endured.

When I finished, he nodded and said, "I know how awful this might sound, but I believe God never intended to heal Allison. I also believe God trusts you a lot, and greatness awaits you if you use this season to go deeper with God and trust Him."

With tears in his eyes, Lawrence switched gears, recalling our first encounter, when Allison and I approached him and his wife and offered to pray for Carol. Out of the many people at their very friendly church, no one, not even those they knew, had ever approached them and offered to pray for her. Instead, they always went up for prayer. Then, two absolute strangers came up to them and lovingly offered to pray. Lawrence said he and Carol never forgot it and carried that encounter in their hearts. How very strange it was for God to bring this man and I together under these circumstances.

"You have a harder journey ahead than me," Lawrence acknowledged.

He had loved his wife for a full and long life. They'd been married for 50 years. I was still young and only got to love my wife for ten years. His children were all grown. I faced an unknown future with a baby boy. He would undoubtedly not change his lifestyle now. Lawrence's time in the world was closer to the end than the beginning. Lawrence shared incredible stories about Carol and some of the encounters she'd had before her death. During the entirety of her battle, he had never left her side. Despite all that happened with his wife, he was very grateful.

That evening, I contemplated the many things Lawrence had said. Judah had fallen asleep while I fed him his nighttime bottle, and I just sat, holding him against me, while I thought about what it all meant. After I laid Judah down in his bed, I did something I had not done in a long time. I took out a piece of a paper, closed my eyes and began to whisper praises to God, as I drew without knowing what I was sketching. The last time I had tried the drawing exercise, our relocation to New Zealand had been set in motion.

I didn't have any particular expectations, but I wanted to do something to try and draw near to God in a way I hadn't for a while. I didn't draw for long but, before I stopped, I whispered to God, "If You want to tell me something through this drawing, let it be what You want to say and not what I want or imagine." If He didn't have anything to say, then I just wanted to see scribbles.

Upon opening my eyes, I immediately saw the profile of a face. The person was looking up and laughing. I could never have replicated the drawing, even if I'd deliberately tried. I thought I had sketched Judah at first glance, but I paused and prayed.

"Holy Spirit, what do you want to tell me?"

I didn't pray or talk to God. I just sat and waited for a

response. Eventually I felt the Holy Spirit say, "Return to the place of childlike trust."

I realized then that I had drawn myself, but with a childish laugh of joy and excitement. I left our room and paced throughout the house. It was late, and the only time the house was quiet. "Return to the place of childlike trust."

I still had so many questions and so much pain, but I felt God calling me back into His arms. Instead of giving me any answers, God simply said, "I'm here, son. Come back to me. Trust me."

Even with my anger and resentment towards God, I wanted to fall into those arms, if for no other reason than because I knew from experience that they felt good. They were a far better prospect than the anguish of grief and bitterness I was in and yet, I resisted them. To surrender to God's embrace meant to trust Him without any justification to do so. Part of me ached to release the pain of my brokenness and the other part clung to the anger and resentment I thought God deserved. Numb from the turmoil within me, I went to my closet and pulled out a box containing some items that Allison had received as gifts that she had especially treasured.

The first item I pulled out was a gift from a woman I'd met at the School of Creativity. Nicola had followed our journey on social media and had sent Allison an art print of one of her original paintings when she was hospitalized. Nicola's paintings usually had a prophetic meaning of some kind. The painting displayed a little girl in a white dress standing in the rain. She had an umbrella that she had tossed on the ground but, instead of seeking shelter from the rain, she was standing in it, uncovered with her arms outstretched, her head lifted, and her eyes closed. A look of surrender was on her face. The attached note said the title of the piece and the meaning: "Standing in the Rain of a Good God. Prophetic meaning: Laying aside our ideas and thoughts of what we think should have been and return to the place of childlike trust. You are God and You are good. I will trust you."

In that moment, I realized that no matter how much I still hurt, and even with all of my reservations and resentment, I still wanted God. I was the best version of myself with Him and I needed Jesus now more than ever. God was never going to give up on me, no matter how much I declared I was through with Him. His relentless efforts to call me home suddenly shattered the walls of hurt and despair that had encased my heart. I could no longer resist the pull of His arms and the comfort of God's presence was suddenly too powerful to reject. My rage subsided and the broken man turned into a boy, desperate for his Heavenly Father, as I cried out to God. I laid on the floor, fell into His arms and wept. I surrendered to the pain of losing Allison, the fear for Judah's safety and the unknowns of the future, but also to the certainty that God was still good and trustworthy. It felt good to be in the arms of Jesus once more.

CHAPTER 39

The weeks carried on with many hard days and the occasional easy day. Judah had the occasional stuffy nose and cough, which always terrified me, but remained generally healthy. The holidays were especially difficult. Seeing other happy families and couples together for the holidays made me long for the everyday joys of being with my spouse.

On Christmas Eve, we watched the evening candlelight service from Koinonia Church on livestream. The church auditorium was not safe for Judah, so we all watched the service together from home. Several of the pastors and their wives spoke.

One of the women began to share the story of Jesus' birth from Joseph and Mary's perspective. "Joseph and Mary had plans for their lives," she said. "Mary's plan was to be married and have a family. Joseph's plan was to have a family and a profession. Yet their plans were drastically interrupted by Jesus' conception. While there was surely joy accompanied in the journey of Jesus's birth, there was also shock. There was frustration that this was not what they had planned. Mary was probably afraid of what her friends and family would think of her because she was pregnant out of wedlock. She no doubt wrestled with embarrassment or even the very real fear of being stoned to death. Mary might have thought about why, when God chose her for greatness, it also meant she had to experience the pain and discomfort of pregnancy and childbirth without first enjoying the pleasure of sex. Further, the change in their plans meant isolation and even endangerment."

"Joseph had his fair share of challenges as well," she continued. "Their circumstances caused initial shame and anger that Mary had betrayed him. He was probably embarrassed in front of his friends and family. His business might have been impacted as their community distanced themselves from them. He carried the knowledge that the child Mary was carrying wasn't his. Further, after surrendering to God's plan for them, they received orders to travel to Bethlehem for a census. At the worst of times, a long, hard journey awaited them. A journey through rough and even dangerous terrain that lasted days and, at the end, Mary went into labor unexpectedly. No one would grant them shelter. The two of them were probably afraid and felt so betrayed by God. God had chosen them for something truly extraordinary and they were met with hardships and relentless difficulties. Nothing about what God had called them to was easy. Surely, they thought, they'd at least have the baby in their home and, instead, Mary was forced to experience childbirth in a barn. She had no choice but to give birth to Immanuel Himself, the King of Kings, in a stable, when she had probably had a specific expectation for that experience in her home in Nazareth. However, instead Mary likely felt degraded and forsaken as she heard the moans of animals around her and smelled feces in the air.

Joseph probably felt like he had failed Mary and Jesus. Maybe he wondered if he had done something wrong or if he had missed a crucial step that could've changed their circumstances. Why did he have to undertake the journey to Bethlehem so late in Mary's pregnancy? Why did the timing of everything unfold the way it did? Why hadn't God intervened to make their circumstances easier and safer? God's timing of events may have felt cruel or even evil. They both probably felt hopeless, alone, and scared; separated from their friends and family, with no one to help them. They suddenly found themselves in a scenario completely beyond their control and considerably short of their plans and expectations."

It all sounded very familiar. Allison and I had surrendered to God's beckoning with a baby on the way and had set off on a scary journey. We were faced with circumstances that defied our every hope and expectation. All our control and plans were lost. We expected Allison to give birth in New Zealand, in our new home, and instead lived in a hospital during the pregnancy and Judah's birth. Judah never came home with both of us to be laid gently in a crib but was instead rushed immediately to the NICU. When he did finally leave the hospital, it was without his mother.

Like Joseph and Mary, I had plans for my life, but God had something entirely different in mind. It felt strange to see that even the caretakers of the Son of God found themselves thrust into the unknown and danger after surrendering to His plans. Even they were not spared fear, doubt and disappointments. Why was that? Why didn't God grant His children favor: clear, safe, tangible favor on their journeys? Why were they so often met with the difficult and the perilous?

My mind wracked with questions as to the nature of the road Joseph and Mary had to walk but was stilled at the incredible way they walked it. Despite their horrible situation, they pressed on, and through their faithfulness the King of Kings entered the world. The circumstances didn't make the situation great...Jesus did. The two of them had dreams and plans, but they had to release control and surrender them, because God had something different planned for them. He was still with them even though His presence may not have been felt. They had to trust God despite not seeing or feeling Him.

Was that what lay ahead? Would I have to walk an agonizing path of mourning a spouse while living in fear that my son's next breath could be his last and yet still trust God was present? How could this all possibly be a part of God's plan? If indeed this was His plan...,why would I want any part of it? What good could come from it? How could God possibly use disease, death, fear and loneliness to usher in something good? How did any of that make Him a God of love?

As I held and stared at a sleeping Judah in my arms, I knew that Joseph and Mary got to see the fruit of their trust as they held a baby Jesus. Was I looking at everything wrong? Was the journey behind and ahead meant to bring Judah safely into the world? Was there more to our story?

I paced the house in tears as numbness consumed me. The joy of my son in my arms as a counterpart to the loss of my wife made my head spin. I was happy and I was hurting. I didn't know whether to thank God for the life He blessed me with or curse Him for the life he stole from me. It was impossible to decide what to think or what to feel. I wondered if Joseph or Mary ever experienced the same?

After Christmas, I received a gift from Nicola. It was a print of a beautiful new painting she had made. On one side were small, withered and dying flowers in a barren field but, from right to left, the flowers became more alive and the field greener and more vibrant. Inside the package was a note explaining that she had made the original painting while praying for healing for Allison and someone else she knew.

Allison never got to see it, and Nicola wondered if, in the end, it was really meant for me. The piece was titled "Glory that Grows in Places of Devastation." The description read, "There are times when we've looked out at the fields of our lives and wondered, could anything ever grow there again? But there is always more to the story. The beauty of redemption, the joy of restoration, and renewed hope. It will come."

On New Year's Eve we took Judah for his first out-of-town trip to Three Rivers, making sure to remain outside and away from any crowds for Judah's safety. Eventually, we drove to the retreat center nearby that Allison and I had visited the year before. My mom and I put Judah in a stroller and walked around the exterior of the main building and along the paved walkways. Judah's eyes were wide with wonder. His gaze consumed every tree, mountain, and bird. My mom then offered to feed Judah and watch him while I spent some time alone and with God.

First, I visited the rooms Allison and I had stayed in. I could vividly remember every moment we had spent there. I paced around outside for a while before going inside the main lobby. The fireplace was roaring with large flames. I remembered sitting in front of that fireplace with Allison. We had longed for a deeper encounter with God and spent time journaling and praying before we played cards and toasted in the new year with cream soda. I treasured the hours we had spent in front of that fireplace.

Suddenly, the retreat's director, whom I had met and talked to during our last visit, appeared.

"Hi, John," I said.

"Joshua! How are you? How's your wife doing?" John

asked.

After I told him what had happened, John sat down with me. "I'm so sorry," he said. He listened as I shared my story with him, and then, shared part of his own journey with me.

"I once was a professional softball player" he began, "until I broke my hip..." He was devastated that he would never play again, but his injury opened the door for him to try painting, which he discovered he loved even more than softball. The retreat center was decorated with several of the stunning paintings he had made.

John then reflected on the time between Jesus's crucifixion and the resurrection. It was a time of grief, fear, and suffering. The followers of Jesus had no idea of the glory that was coming or what was being birthed from that suffering.

"God does not waste suffering," he said. "I believe God is going to spark a hopeful fire in you through this suffering that will spread to others, but first you have to allow the flames to cauterize the wound in your heart that is still so clearly bleeding. Though a scar may remain, it carries with it a story."

As we prayed together, I asked God to cauterize the wound in my heart. Eventually, I got up from the fireplace and walked along the trail that Allison and I had walked during our visit. It led to a small bench surrounded by Manzanita trees. I stood and stared at where Allison and I had sat together and prayed for our future. We were excited, scared, but also filled with hope.

As soon as I sat on the bench and turned my gaze towards the beautiful Sierra Nevada Mountains, a hawk flew directly over my head. I was startled at first, but then at peace. I was ready to return to the place of childlike trust that God had been calling me to and, in doing so, I knew I would rise to new heights.

I thought of the springboard analogy that Roger Watson had shared with Allison and I the day we left for New Zealand. We had to go low before going up, he'd said. There had been many reiterations of that prophetic word from others and from God Himself recently. I had certainly gone low, and I was ready to go up.

"Here we go," I said, as I stood up.

Back at home, I stayed up and waited for midnight to come on my own. The year of the whirlwind was coming to a close. Everything about the future was a mystery to me. I had no plans, only expectations. I looked forward to seeing Judah strengthen and grow. It was a delightful thought for the two of us to finally venture out into the world. I had no plans to start writing, but my interest in finishing Allison's book had been renewed.

Quietly, I watched a countdown as 2015 ended and I prayed for the coming year. I hoped I would draw closer to God and experience trust in Him, without borders. As the countdown ended and 2016 began, I thanked God for the victories that we did experience and everything good I could think of that had happened in 2015.

It didn't take long for thoughts of the many tragedies, pains, and losses to set in. My fists rose up and shook. I forced myself to stop what I was doing. It was so easy for me to focus on all that I had lost instead of what I still had. If I pitied myself, it would only lead to more pain. I didn't need any more sadness and depression in my life. What I needed was happiness and joy. Judah needed that from me, too. He needed a dad who smiled, laughed, and played, not one who moped, cried, and wallowed in despair. I had to be the best version of myself for the people I loved. The only way I could become that was by being grateful. Gratitude was the key.

I began journaling. There was a lot to write about from all that had happened, but I began with writing Allison's favorite Bible verse: Ephesians 3:20 "Now all glory to God who is able, through his mighty power at work within us, to accomplish infinitely more than we might ask or think." I then began writing things I was thankful for. I thanked God that Allison and I got to spend so much time together during our marriage. We not only loved each other, but truly enjoyed being with one another, collaborating and sharing our lives. I was grateful that we'd had the means to travel as much as we did and that our last days before entering into that terrible battle were spent in one of the most beautiful places on earth. I gave thanks that Allison got to see that Judah was healthy before she died and that we had one professional photo shoot together before the end.

It was a strange feeling since there was so much to be upset about, but I felt lighter and happier the more I listed all I was thankful for. The more I wrote, the more I realized all there was to be thankful for. I was grateful Allison didn't die alone that night when she had no pulse and was revived. Instead, she was surrounded by family when the end came. Thankfulness poured out from me as I praised God for all of the wonderful and dedicated staff that cared for Allison and Judah. I wasn't bankrupt from medical bills and essentially had no financial concerns. I was in a home filled with love and people to help me and Judah. While my community could indeed be overbearing at times, they were there for me if I needed anything at all. I thanked God that Allison and I could be together and with Judah the entire time she was at Stanford and especially that we caught the disease in time for Allison to save Judah's life. Finally, I sang praises and thanks that God had continually reached out to me and called me back into His arms.

My words and song quietly filled the room for almost an hour. God had directed my every step in 2015 and, even though my current destination was not where I wanted to be, and my companion no longer walked with me, I knew I didn't walk the path alone.

At long last I couldn't think of anything else to say, so I just worshipped God before walking down the hallway and into my room. Judah was sleeping soundly and peacefully. Bending down, I kissed my son on his head.

"I'm grateful for you, Judah Aslan Cordero. I love you. Happy New Year."

CHAPTER 40

Since Judah had been born, I only left my parents' home twice for overnight trips: once when I spread Allison's ashes on our anniversary and the second time when I traveled to a healing conference in Northern California, hosted by an international minister named Randy Clark. I had gone seeking to understand why God heals sometimes and other times He doesn't.

In one session titled, "The Thrill of Victory," Randy shared stories of the times he'd prayed for people and they were miraculously healed. The next session, however, was titled "The Agony of Defeat" and contained heart wrenching accounts of times he had prayed for people who weren't healed.

In one story, Randy shared about a small deaf girl he'd prayed for over the course of three days. At the conclusion of that time the girl was still deaf. When it was obvious God wasn't going to heal her, the girl buried her face in her mother's stomach and wept. The girl had a disease that caused her deafness. The disease eventually spread to her other senses and destroyed them one by one before consuming her brain entirely and killing her. The entire audience was weeping.

The session could be summed up in three words. *We don't know.* Randy didn't know why God healed some and not others, nor why we sometimes experience miracles and other times we don't. I appreciated that Randy didn't try to justify or rationalize anything with guesses.

While much had been said about healing and what the Bible said about it, I still didn't have any clear answers. I knew

God loved all His children. Healings and miracles didn't revolve around His favoritism or lack of it, but what do you say to someone who has suffered an unbearable tragedy? How do you justify God being a God of love in the midst of disease and death?

God put on my heart Isaiah 64:8 which says, "But now, O Lord, you are our Father; we are the clay, and you are our potter; we are all the work of your hand." I remembered the words Bobby Hill spoke to Allison and me years before. "...Never question the Potter's intentions." God wasn't really giving an answer to my questions at all. Rather, He was reminding me that He was still sovereign no matter the experience or outcome and, even without any answers, He wanted me to continue to have childlike trust. It wasn't my responsibility to justify God, only to trust Him.

When the session concluded, Randy prayed for the audience. "God wants to bring forth breakthrough for those in agony from defeat," he said.

As I prayed to receive God's peace, the words, "Reckless Love and Ridiculous Hope" burned into my mind. Different individuals walked through the auditorium praying for people. I had my eyes closed as I prayed, and heard a woman approach me.

She touched my forehead and said, "Reckless love, Jesus!"

It felt as if an electrical current surged through me and I could no longer stand. Since Allison had died, I had a very difficult time picturing our lives before the hospital. When I tried to think of Allison, my thoughts were pulled to her in the ICU or her dying in my arms. Abundant joy-filled memories suddenly sprang forth. It was like a dam had been built up in my mind, holding back all of the happiness of the past and God had suddenly brought it smashing down. I had heard of the term, "Drunk in the spirit" before and it always seemed a little strange to me, but I was experiencing just that. I laughed, uncontrollably. I cried from laughing so hard and so much. Joy was coursing through me and out of me like I had never experienced before.

Another hand touched me, and a man's voice said, "God's marking you, brother."

For quite some time, I couldn't get up. When I finally did, I worshiped God and felt the Holy Spirit say, "Worship is both your weapon and how you will draw near to me during this season."

I had a revelation in that moment. When we lift our arms in worship, we make a physical gesture of surrender. We're releasing our control, doubt, fear, and disbelief. We're choosing to thank God for all He has done and acknowledging His power and splendor. It is only when we come to a place of surrender that we truly know any semblance of victory in life, even in the midst of defeat. The only difference between a physical gesture of surrender and victory is a fist versus an open hand. In either case, your arms are still outstretched. Just a simple change of an open hand indicates a huge difference. Surrender is the path to peace, contentment, and victory.

I remembered what God had told me on that unforgettable night on New Year's Eve 2014. He not only told me to surrender my plans for the future, but to have an expectation for it. I went to a healing conference for answers and instead of going home with them, I left my questions behind. I released my need for clarity and control and accepted my life was not about me. I had surrendered once again.

More firsts came and went without Allison, including her thirtieth birthday. In an effort to carry on Allison's generous spirit, I decided to do something for others, strangers especially, to celebrate her life. One of Allison's favorite things to do for her birthday was to sign up for as much free stuff as possible, since many stores gave away discounts or free items and food on your birthday. She especially loved getting a free venti Frappuccino from Starbucks. Inspired by that, I purchased thirty $5 gift cards and began passing them out to strangers on Allison's birthday. In addition, I gave a large gift card to the manager at a local Starbucks and asked him to treat as many people as he could before it ran out. He let me put up a sign at the register honoring Allison. It was fun seeing people's expressions as they received their free coffee, and I had the opportunity to share about Allison's story and legacy with a number of people.

In the days and weeks that followed, I had many opportunities to share about Allison's story. One day, after one of those opportunities, I arrived home to a silent house. I sat down quietly for a few moments before getting up to check on Judah. Upon entering the bedroom, I saw Allison sitting up on the bed holding a sleeping Judah.

"Hey you two," I whispered.

Allison looked up at me and smiled. She mouthed, "Hey" back.

Her hair was starting to grow back, but it was a different color, something her team in hematology said could happen. I leaned into Allison and gently kissed her.

"He just dozed off," Allison whispered.

"How's he been?" I asked.

"Oh, he was great once I started feeding him," Allison answered.

I smiled. "Anything you want to do today? Do you want to get out of the house later?"

Allison thought for a moment and said, "A walk in the park would be nice. I really want to take a nap first though."

"How about I take Judah and you can have a nap now?" I asked.

"Are you sure?"

"Of course. I'll hold him on the couch and watch some TV or something while he sleeps."

"Okay, sounds good," Allison said, while gently handing our sleeping son over to me.

Judah looked incredibly content and peaceful.

"I love you," I said to Allison.

Allison lifted her index finger and bent it down and up twice.

I winked at her and tip-toed out of the room, but not before glancing back at Allison, who watched us and smiled.

I gasped as I woke suddenly from the dream.

Since Allison's birthday, I had been dreaming of her often in different scenarios that felt like alternate realities in a science fiction movie. I dreamt of various outcomes where she had lived and was discharged from Stanford. In many ways, they were similar to how I expected life would be after her discharge. My dreams were the closest things I had to memories of us together outside the hospital and in a home.

I let out an uncomfortable moan. The dream was so

beautiful but painful to wake up from. It had felt so real. I longed to return to the world of the dream and stay with my wife, but I couldn't fall back asleep.

A few close friends and family had been dreaming of Allison as well. My mother shared a vision she'd had of Allison when we attended a worship night at church. She saw Allison with her hair long and a big smile. She looked incredible and was dancing with complete and utter delight. In the vision, Allison looked directly at my mother and, although she didn't say anything, the expression on her face said it all. She was happy. It was as if Allison was saying don't worry about me. I'm just fine.

Stephanie, a friend and client of mine, also reached out to me. She had experienced a vision of Allison and wanted to share it with me in person. Stephanie flew all the way from Las Vegas just to speak with me. Allison had worked directly with her on several videos prior to our relocation. Stephanie shared that she had seen Allison in front of a stunning house on top of a hill. Instinctively, she knew the house was Allison's home in heaven and she was delighted to be living there. The unique architecture melded with beautiful landscaping and made a synthesis of the two. Grass and dirt covered the roof of the large house, lush vines scaled over the walls and flowers of all colors and sizes occupied the front. It was as if the house itself were alive. Stephanie described the exact characteristics of Bilbo Baggins' house that Allison and I had seen in New Zealand and the cottage we saw in a photograph in the halls of Stanford Hospital. Allison had said she wanted a house just like it one day.

Allison's friend, Melissa, sent me a message of a vision

she had experienced. She said, "I was just praying for you, Josh, and got the image of you sitting on a patch of beautiful green grass with Judah sleeping beside you. Sadness was all over your face. What you couldn't see was that Allie was behind you with her hand on your back and Jesus, in all His shining light, had His arms around you both! He truly knows every tear you've cried, and He loves you and your little family so much! You are loved! 'You keep track of all my sorrows, you have collected all of my tears in Your bottle. You have recorded each one in Your book.' Psalms 56:8."

It was a comforting message, but I couldn't help but wonder why so many people were having dreams and visions of Allison?

The weeks continued to roll by and with them came more special occasions. Mother's Day was especially difficult for me. I made a video tribute to Allison called, "The Mother Who Surrendered All". In it, I opened up about my grief and Allison's sacrifice. It seemed so unfair to me that she placed the wellbeing of her son before her own but never got to enjoy a Mother's Day with her child in her arms. As I spoke to the camera and recounted all that Allison had experienced and accomplished, it seemed almost unbelievable. It was an especially strange thought to know that Allison was in Heaven with Eliana and I was with Judah.

Over the weeks and months since his birth, Judah had endured so many tests and exams that even I was exhausted from them all. High risk assessments were implemented to evaluate his cognitive abilities, more scans were done of his brain and I took him to one specialist after another to ensure he was healthy. Judah had crushed just about every single milestone and limitation placed on him. His immune system was building up and nearly everything checked out perfectly with one major exception: his ureter.

The ureter is a tube that connects the kidney to the bladder and allows urine to pass through and eventually expel it. Judah's left ureter had a kink in it and fluid was backing up in his body. Judah had to experience an invasive and grueling test where a catheter was inserted in his penis and dye was injected in his body through an IV. Judah screamed and screamed during the process and kept looking at me as if to save him from his pain. It was horrible. The test revealed there was no way the kink would come undone on its own when Judah grew, as it did with some boys. He'd need surgery soon or risk his kidney being permanently damaged. A surgeon would need to laparoscopically cut out the kinked portion of Judah's ureter and fuse the two exposed sides together with a stint. A second procedure would have to happen weeks after that to remove the stint. Upon hearing the news, I cried for days and was filled with terror.

Judah was just a little over eight months old when he was put to sleep for his surgery. I anxiously paced in the waiting room and prayed for God's grace and favor to be in the surgical room and upon his surgeons.

After three agonizing hours, Judah's doctor emerged and told us the procedure had gone well and was "completely textbook". Judah was discharged before the end of the following day, but he had a rough recovery. The tracheal tube from the surgery had left his throat raw and sore. Every time he cried, drank his bottle, or even giggled, it hurt him badly. Slowly, things improved, and routines resumed.

My good friend David Watson visited regularly. David recognized that I was at another low point and suggested I go out of town with him for a few days. As we considered our options, I discovered that an event was taking place soon, an event with special meaning at a familiar place.

David accompanied me as I returned to Bethel Church for the 2016 School of Creativity.

CHAPTER 41

Driving uphill past the many flag poles and onto the Bethel Church campus felt like coming home. The theme for the week was "Imagine" and the main image, I discovered, was of a woman dancing in worship. Paintings and sketches of a woman worship dancing decorated the walls. I couldn't help thinking how coincidental that was, and it made me think of Allison's love for worship.

As I worshiped during the morning session, God spoke to me. "You need to put the pen of your life in my hands. I am re-writing your identity."

With all that had transpired, I based my identity on all I had lost. In my eyes, I was little more than a widower and a single father. It was a sad identity, and one still filled with despair. I wept because being in the presence of God was overwhelming.

I asked him, "What are you writing me into?"

He said, "The one."

I had believed for a long time that God was the ultimate creative person. He speaks to us in unique ways and does things that force us outside of the limitations we place on Him. Immediately, I had a mental picture in my head of Neo from *The Matrix* movie franchise. While I am a huge fan of the series, and its Biblical analogies are very intriguing, I thought what I was experiencing was stupid. There was no way God was actually comparing me to a character in a movie! It had to be an experience of my own design and imagination! So, I dismissed it.

As the day continued, I visited several of the prophetic booths, where artists prayed for me and asked about my life, before painting or drawing something prophetic for me. I deliberately tried to avoid going into detail about all that had happened the previous year, but the questions they asked made it impossible. Each artist I spoke with wept and was astonished by all that had happened. I was encouraged by their profound words and the day became filled with many incredible experiences.

In the late afternoon, I noticed a young woman. She, like many others, was part of a ministry team available to pray with attendees and create something prophetic for them. I already had received several items but felt like I was supposed to sit down with her. Her name was Michelle. She was from Canada and was a student at Bethel's School of Supernatural Ministry. After praying, Michelle asked a few questions, so I went ahead and shared about Allison, Judah, and the journey we had all taken. She paused, listened for what God was putting on her heart and then began to draw with her colored pencils. My heart raced when I realized what she was drawing. It was Neo from the *The Matrix*. I hadn't shared anything with Michelle about what had happened earlier that morning.

Michelle asked me if I had seen *The Matrix* before.

"Yes," I said, smiling.

"So, this is a scene from *The Matrix* where Neo realizes the power that he has. I just saw you in that position. You're stopping the bullets, taking authority, and saying 'No'. I now see things for how they are. I see the reality of my situation. I'm taking control of it and I will no longer allow my circumstances to get the better of me.' You can see into the

Heavenly places. Does that make sense?"

I laughed and told her what had happened to me earlier that day.

She also laughed as she exclaimed, "Wow! That's so awesome!"

I had experienced a new anointing that morning and didn't even realize it. My story was about more than what I had lost. It was also about all I had gained in Christ. Even though the enemy had launched scores of horrendous bullets at me and my family, God had given me the ability to say, "No", and they would be deflected. My identity was not as a widower or as a single dad. I now saw myself as God saw me. Experiences that should have permanently broken me, God was able to take, remake and rewrite into what He wanted.

David beamed with excitement for me as I told him about all that had happened. I was so glad we had come. Two years before, in this very place, a journey began. A journey that led Allison and I to making a movie, getting pregnant, moving to New Zealand, battling a ferocious disease, death, and now, starting over. It was meaningful and healing to be there again.

The next day I bumped into one of the prophetic artists I had met. She insisted I go to a testimonial table where people could write down what they had experienced at the School of Creativity, so Bethel could chronicle the things that God was doing. Making my way to the table, I saw cards available to write on, but they had just a few short lines. A man behind the table approached me as I laughed at the card.

He looked at me inquisitively and I said, "There's just no way I can share all that happened on these."

He asked me to elaborate, so I told him about the previous two years and my encounters the day before. The man was stunned. He agreed that the cards weren't big enough and asked if he could record a video of me summarizing what I had shared with him. I said yes, assuming he just wanted to chronicle my testimony. When we finished, he surprised me by saying he wanted to share the video with Theresa Dedmon, the woman who managed the School of Creativity and the Creative Arts department at Bethel Church.

Not long after, I connected with my friend Nicola. Though she'd sent multiple paintings, it had been over two years since we'd seen each other. When we finished speaking, I held out my phone to take a photo of us together when a text popped up on my screen.

"Hi Joshua - It's Theresa Dedmon. I am so excited about your testimony. Would you be willing to share it after worship tonight at the School of Creativity?"

Nicola was beside me as I read the text. "That's amazing!" she said.

I was speechless. I pictured Roger Watson standing before Allison and me the day we left for New Zealand. While I had contemplated many times the springboard analogy he'd shared with us, I had never given much thought to what he had said just after that. He'd said that one day we would speak at the events and places that had helped guide us on our journey. Now, our story would touch people in the same manner that we had been touched at Bethel Church.

As my journey had caused me to do countless times, I cried. I was overwhelmed at the realization that Roger's prophecy was coming to life and that I was being given the honor to speak at Bethel Church and share Allison's legacy of love and the journey we had walked.

That very evening, I stood on the stage of Bethel Church and shared our story. The audience exclaimed, laughed, and cried as I recounted everything from God telling me about Judah and what his name meant, to New Zealand and Allison's death.

As I spoke, a beautiful feather fell in front of me. I'd heard accounts of feathers falling out of thin air as indicators of the presence of angelic beings, but I had never experienced anything like it firsthand. For a moment, I was speechless and didn't know what to do or say in response, so I just continued my story.

The audience rose with cheering and clapping twice before I had even finished. When I shared about what had happened the day before, when God told me that He was writing a new identity for me, everyone cheered again. Theresa held up Michelle's confirming drawing of Neo for the audience to see. I concluded by mentioning *Surrendering All* and that I believed God had finally activated me to finish writing the book Allison had begun. The audience rose once more and applauded as I left the stage.

It took everything I had not to break down. My heart was so full in that moment. I hoped that I had honored Allison with what I had shared.

Nicola texted me just after I spoke and said, "That was massive! Crazy courage. A story of reckless love and ridiculous hope...beautifully done Josh. A privilege to watch and hear. Heaven stood up to watch."

A woman named Patricia King was the speaker that

evening. I hadn't heard of her before, but was told she was a renowned prophetic evangelist. Her words were captivating and powerful. Near the end of her message, she spoke about the times when you're in a place you have nothing left and don't know how to keep moving forward.

"There are some of you who are pressing on no matter what. You have told God, "Yes" and are going to move forward. Don't let go no matter what it takes. When you've come to that place of perseverance, you've stepped into an authoritative realm."

Patricia then said, "I don't know if Joshua is still in this room tonight but...are you still here, Joshua?"

I waved my arm in the air for her to see.

Patricia continued, "Joshua, I was so touched by your story. My heart is broken for you in many ways and yet the word of the Lord to you is so powerful. I felt the Lord say to you, Joshua, I am going to give you the spoils of this battle. You have paid a big price. You know the warfare. You really know the warfare. He's saying to you to not give up and keep moving forward because He's given you this word that you can stand on. You have a brand-new clean slate and He's saying, 'Get excited about each day.' It's just one little step at a time and then another little step at a time. The Lord says, 'It's going to be different than it was and it's going to be different than what you think, but it's going to be effective. Just rejoice in each little step along the way. He loves you. He loves you so much."

The audience erupted in applause and cheers. When Patricia finished, swarms of people gathered around me to share how much my testimony had touched them. Some shared prophetic words with me and some even gave me money for Judah's future. One woman handed me $1,000 and said God told her to give it to someone who honored Him in a big way. She said she had a very specific person in mind that was on Bethel Church's staff, but God told her that Judah was going to bring Him even more honor than that person. I laughed and cried at all the things I was told.

After forty-five minutes, it was clear conversations with people could go on for a long time, but I felt that I was supposed to call it a night. David led me out of the crowd. By the time we returned and settled into our hotel rooms, it was after midnight. It was also my birthday. I had just turned thirty-one.

The next morning, David and I returned to Bethel Church, where I was continuously overwhelmed by people coming up to me. I was delighted that Allison's story was touching so many people in such profound ways.

During the morning session, Theresa Dedmon spoke and was giving out gifts to random people in the audience. She held up a necklace and said, "I feel like I'm supposed to give this to someone whose birthday is today."

David and my other friends waved and yelled, "It's Joshua's birthday!"

"It's your birthday, Joshua?" Theresa asked surprised.

I nodded.

"Really?" She asked again.

"Yes," I said, laughing.

"Get up here!" Theresa said.

I walked up onto the stage again and she handed me a necklace that had a key and a pendant attached to it. The pendant had one word on it: "Transform."

"Wow," I said, as I held up the necklace and told the audience that two years before when Allison and I were at the School of Creativity, Shawn Bolz had prophesied that he saw keys in our hands.

Between sessions, David and I found a secluded area to escape the crowds. We began to eat lunch but spotted a young woman that seemed like she wanted to approach us but was shy about it.

"That woman's lurking," David said, laughing.

I waved at the woman and said, "Hello! How's it going?"

The woman laughed shyly and approached me.

Her name was Anna. She had come to the School of Creativity with her husband, Trevor, and was pregnant with their second child. Anna shared that she was a nurse and painted frequently as a gift to other moms. She asked if she could paint Allison as a gift to me and Judah. I excitedly accepted the offer and we exchanged information.

The rest of our time at Bethel Church was extraordinary. I had had no expectations for our time there and in some ways had been very put off about the idea of even attending. I shook my head at the thought of what I might have missed.

"Thank you, God. Thank you for all you've done and all you're doing."

CHAPTER 42

As soon as I returned home, I started writing
Surrendering All: A Story of Reckless Love and Ridiculous Hope.
For the first time, the reality of just how daunting the task was
going to be set in. We both had journaled extensively, and I
had hundreds of pages chronicling all that had happened. Raw
and painful moments to romantic and thrilling adventures.
Thousands of social media posts, photos, and video clips
captured every single step of our journey. I had no shortage of
material to pull from where my memory might fail, but could I
endure combing through the details of everything we'd been
through?

It didn't take long for the process to become
overwhelming. I had written less than a thousand words before
realizing I wasn't ready and shelved the endeavor. The pages of
our journals contained too many memories I was terrified to
relive.

"How am I ever going to do this?" I asked myself, as I
slid Allison's journal back onto the bookshelf. Even after all the
positive things that had happened in the previous few weeks, I
could feel myself slipping. I was once again at a crossroads
where I could easily walk down the path of bitterness and
sadness.

I began to flip through my Bible and came upon the
account of Shadrach, Meshach, and Abednego. At the time King
Nebuchadnezzar had set up a golden idol and ordered all of the
kingdom to bow down before it. When he received word that
Shadrack, Meshach and Abednego refused to obey his

command, he ordered them to be brought before him. King Nebuchadnezzar threatened to throw the men in a fiery furnace if they did not comply. In response, the men said, "If we are thrown into the blazing furnace, the God we serve is able to deliver us from it, and He will deliver us from Your Majesty's hand but even if He does not, we want you to know, Your Majesty, that we will not serve your gods or worship the image of gold you have set up."

The three of them knew God had the power to save them but acknowledged there was the possibility He wouldn't. Yet, this left them undeterred. They had chosen to love and obey God regardless of the outcome, even if that meant their horrible deaths. While I had read the story before, the significance of their choice had not occurred to me. Those men had surrendered everything, with no hope or expectation of a favorable outcome. They were determined to remain faithful no matter what. They ended up miraculously surviving their encounter with death. Allison had not. All of them shared the same level of faith.

My thoughts turned to wondering what Allison was doing that very moment. Did she have any regrets or disappointment in God? While I knew Allison was indeed happy in Heaven, I couldn't help wondering what she did there. I didn't think those in heaven just sat around eating fruit, playing harps, and worshipping God twenty-four-seven. What was it like for Allison?

Just a few days later I received a message from my friend, Vanessa (who had given Allison the beach magnet as well as many other gifts).

"Hey Josh. I wanted to share something with you. I'm

twelve weeks pregnant today and had the first ultrasound yesterday; there was no heartbeat, and they estimate the baby passed away three weeks ago. This morning as I awoke and grieved my current reality, and began to wonder where my baby is, as it is here with me physically, but not here, the Holy Spirit showed me a vision. I saw beautiful Allie; hair long and flowing, big loose curls and a flowered headband, pearly beautiful skin, and a white dress. She was sitting, rocking a baby and there were numerous others around her sitting, playing, laughing. She was so filled with joy and at peace. My heart believes my baby is there with her. I feel like God wants you to know that Allison is at peace because her life's mission of bringing Judah into this world was successfully completed, and she knows he is in good hands here. And the work she is doing in heaven is of such great importance. The babies who have been lost before they have been known need a mommy to love and care for them, and I know that is what she is doing. Though I grieve so greatly, my heart feels some relief. I hope this helps you in some way as well. She is missed, but such an important piece of God's plan."

When I finished reading Vanessa's message, my heart was bursting and my face was wet with tears. Allison wanted to be a mother more than anything and, while she didn't get to experience motherhood in her earthly life, she certainly was in Heaven. I couldn't even begin to imagine all of the reunions she would get to witness as infants and children that perished are reunited with their parents, some perhaps even meeting for the first time. I couldn't think of anything that would make her happier. It wouldn't surprise me if she taught them all to worship dance. It was interesting to me that the more I chose to trust God, the more I saw grace where I had thought there was none.

God's grace continued to show itself in new and surprising ways.

Anna, the nurse who wanted to do a painting of Allison, had kept in touch and asked if I could share some videos and photos of Allison with her. Over time, she created a watercolor painting of Allison holding Judah and mailed it to me shortly before Judah's first birthday. I had intentionally asked her not to show me anything until it was finished. As I slid the painting out of its package and unrolled it, I was speechless. Anna had recreated Allison's likeness perfectly. In the painting, Allison was smiling and beaming with joy at the smiling baby she held in her arms. It was exactly how I imagined the two of them together: healthy and happy.

I suddenly realized it was the closest thing I had to a photograph of Allison, with hair, holding Judah. By the time Judah was born, Allison had already lost all of her hair from the chemotherapy, and either she or Judah always had some kind of medical equipment attached to them in every photo I had of them together. But not this. This was a masterpiece and instantly became another family heirloom. It was a tribute to the love and joy Allison still carried in her heart as a mommy. Even though Judah and I were separated from her, we could rest assured that we would be together again one day. It was a reminder of the miracle of Christ's love and how nothing can separate us from it. Not even death.

A note accompanied the painting with its name and a short summary. Anna called it, "Greater Love." In the description, she wrote, "You know that feeling of solemn joy when you rest under a massive tree? The way that you feel mournful, and yet somehow still overwhelmed by beauty as you watch willowy branches moving in an invisible wind? You can almost feel the beauty and the sadness sung by the rustling, brilliant leaves. It's intangible, but so close. To Allison, the invisible is seen. She leans on the solid chest of a completely tangible God. Last year, this mother chose a love that cost her life. She chose to delay life-saving leukemia treatment to give her unborn son a chance to live. Her little boy now has an endlessly bright future due to his mother's sacrifice and his dad's enduring care. One photo caught my attention as I watched a slideshow of Allison's story. I was struck by the confidence and peace in her eyes as she leaned on her husband's chest. Clearly, she felt safe there. I see her in a similar place now: leaning on the safest and strongest chest in the world. I see her at peace in the arms of the Father, knowing the love that she believed in for so long. Knowing that love is enough for the family she loves on earth."

A few weeks later, family and friends, including nurse Melissa from Stanford, gathered together from several different states to participate in Judah's first birthday party. What a celebration it was! My father said it was the happiest he'd seen me in a long time. We all laughed, opened presents and Judah had cake for the first time, which he happily devoured. We had a massive pool party, and everyone took photos of Judah and wanted to love on the miracle boy of the hour. I couldn't believe how big he was getting and how much he looked like Allison already. He was a living embodiment of her words that, "We need to be people who have so much hope it's ridiculous." Even at just one-year-old, Judah displayed courage and strength that rivaled his mother's.

As I watched Judah splashing in the pool water, I thought of the times that lay ahead. No doubt there would be paths filled with challenges, mystery, and adventures. It wouldn't have been that long ago that those thoughts would've made me afraid. Not now, though. I was now filled with hope because of God's enduring grace and the fact that my son was with me. I had Judah to take with me on the journey of life and because of that, I had courage; courage that whatever happened, we'd have each other. Judah had very much healed my heart and restored my joy. His life and story did the same for so many. I am so proud of him.

While there had been plenty of hard days and some very low moments that accompanied parenthood, Judah brought me so much hope and delight. Many times, I ranted that the wrong parent had died. I thought Judah deserved better than me. He deserved his mother. Allison loved him more than her own life. How intensely she prayed for him over the years before he was even conceived. Allison loved children dearly. She was the parent Judah deserved, not me. Yet God chose me to raise him. It made little sense to me, but I felt privileged and humbled to parent this incredible little boy.

As we celebrated Judah's birthday, it was more than just a celebration of his life; it was a celebration that I got to be part of it.

After being a full-time single dad for over a year I decided to reopen my freelance filmmaking business and started offering photography as well. Since I had absolutely no debt and my community had raised tens of thousands of dollars for me, I had the means to purchase equipment and begin working in my profession again. After twenty months of living with my parents; Judah, Lilo and I moved into a home of our own. My business thrived and grew even larger than when Allison and I ran things together. Judah had finished all of his evaluations and overall was strong and healthy. We slowly made our way back into the social world, although it was definitely difficult for both of us to adjust. Life was not without its many difficulties.

Continuing to be a single dad and self-employed was incredibly challenging and parenting in general was harder than I ever imagined. While there were many highs, there were plenty of lows as well. For far too long, I returned to a path of discontentment.

Tarry's movie had been successful, and he and his family relocated to another country. My friends Mark and Becky became pregnant again, but this time with twins. I saw many of our dreams and goals lived out in the lives of the people closest to me and I hated it.

The many activations I experienced from my time at Bethel Church had withered. Nearly everything Lawrence had told me I had shut out of my mind. For over two years I barely touched *Surrendering All*. Whether because of procrastination, the pain of reliving past experiences or something else entirely, I barely made any progress.

It had been almost three years since Allison had died and the pain of her absence persisted. I had retreated from an intimate life with God. The daily decision to choose joy and gratefulness was far more challenging than being bitter, so I abandoned the effort entirely. In many ways I was spiritually dead. In my efforts to numb my emptiness, I had eaten compulsively over the last year and gotten hooked on pornography. Judah would be starting preschool soon and the thought of not having him around the house during the day left me sad. He was one of the few things that made me happy, and I loved being around him. I struggled with guilt because I knew he wasn't getting the best version of me.

On August 14, 2018, I was alone in my home for the night. I had finished a photography job that went late, and my parents had Judah. After I transferred the photos I had captured onto my computer, I sat on the couch and began to feel sorry for myself once again. For a reason beyond my comprehension, I decided to watch the "Journey of Healing" videos that Allison and I had made when she was hospitalized. I hadn't seen them in years, and I began to watch them all, one after another. I saw a family struggling in the fight of their lives and yet filled with so much hope and determination. Their faith seemed so naive to me.

Tarry had once told me, "Faith isn't proven by the end result. It's proven by the condition of our hearts. The words we speak and the actions we take. We are only responsible for our end of the deal. She (Allison) was a champion of faith and an example to us all. What's the alternative? Accept the facts? No way! We do that and it kills our faith. Allison died a hero. A hero of faith."

Tarry's words echoed in my thoughts and then I came upon part five of the video series that Allison and I titled, "Emotional Days." I watched a worn and tired Allison share about how the first round of chemotherapy failed and that her hair was starting to fall out. Despite this, while Allison was feeling low and even crying, it was so obvious that her resolve had not been broken. My wife looked at me through the camera and said, "I think it'd be so easy in this situation to just spiral downward, and we just have to have hope. We have to be a people that have so much hope it's ridiculous. I just want to have that kind of hope. It's what's keeping us going. That's just what we have to cling to. The alternative is just to pity myself and just hate the situation I'm in and that would make things miserable. So, I choose to have hope and I choose to have a good attitude and I choose to fight."

I wept uncontrollably. I longed to have the faith that Allison had and that I once possessed. A yearning burned in me to finally stop stumbling in a cycle of resentment, jealousy, sadness, pity, and bitterness and just have hope. Ridiculous hope.

I began to worship God and paced throughout the house until I came upon the three vases that I had purchased for Allison. It had been a long time since I had gone through them, so I reached for the vase that contained the things Allison had written that she was praying for. My fingers reached into the opening and I grabbed the first paper and held it up. It said, "A new heart" in my handwriting. The date said, "September 15, 2015." At that point, Allison was too weak to write, and that morning she had asked me to write for her. That night she had died.

A long time had passed since I heard God speak to me but, in that moment, I felt God say with absolute clarity, "I will give you a new heart right now if you ask for it."

"Yes, please!" I shouted. "I need a new heart, Jesus!" I cried out and wept.

I could feel every single negative emotion I had been

clinging to slip off me. It was like I was undergoing spiritual surgery. Gratitude returned, hope filled me, and praises emanated from my lips. The months and months of shame and regret from running from God subsided and I felt at home in God's loving embrace once again.

Spread out on several shelves were the Willow Tree figurines I had purchased for Allison over the years. They were one of the few things she kept when we sold our belongings to relocate to New Zealand. I found myself staring at the two figures I had purchased for Allison on her twenty-ninth birthday. They were the last birthday present I had ever given her. One was of a woman with her arms extended high in a victorious pose. Angelic wings were mounted on her back. The other was of a man sitting down and bent over reading a book. He was sitting on a pile of books and in front of him were even more books. When I had seen the two figures side by side in the store, I knew I was supposed to purchase them for Allison. But now, in this moment, I realized they were meant for me as much as for Allison. I had unknowingly prophesied over Allison and I through her birthday present. The angelic woman represented a victorious Allison who had accomplished what she set out to do by saving the life of her son. Even in death, Allison was celebrated and honored as a victor. The man was me, pouring over the journals we had both written to tell a story. Our story.

Immediately, I grabbed my laptop and began to write. In just two hours I wrote more than I had written in over two years. As I flipped through the pages of our journals, I no longer cried. Instead, I took notes and continued to write very late into the night. While I had dabbled on our book over the years, now I was officially writing it.

Just eight days later Judah and I stood in front of Future Hope Preschool for his first day of school. The very same preschool where Allison had taught the children to worship dance when she was pregnant with Judah. I was a flood of emotions and Judah was clearly nervous. He had gotten so big, and despite his reservations there was also a curiosity in his big blue eyes.

We prayed together and I quoted Joshua 1:9 to him, "Be strong and courageous, Judah!"

I told him I loved him; kissed and hugged him fiercely.

In a single moment, yet another new season of our lives had begun. After Judah was settled in his new class, I walked across the street and sat on the curb. I cried for what felt like a long time. While I was so happy for Judah, it seemed so unfair to send him off to school without Allison doing it with me. Once again, I could feel the feelings of bitterness, sadness and anger rise in me. This wasn't the life I wanted for myself or Judah. I didn't want our journey to end the way it had.

My head lifted up and I looked out across the street at Judah's preschool. I saw a large banner that displayed the name of the preschool in colorful letters: "Future Hope". The name felt especially fitting in that moment. I thought of the saying that "Time heals all wounds." It was a complete and total lie. I had come to realize that time acts the same towards a great emotional wound as it does to a physical one. If a wound is left to time without being treated, it becomes infected. The wound will worsen, and the infection will spread to the rest of the body, poisoning and breaking it down. You have to choose to go to a physician and decide to receive treatment.

Choice is ultimately what heals us. Choosing to find joy over sadness, to hope when there is only cause for despair, and to focus on what has been gained instead of what has been lost. There is no single defining moment, encounter or activation that permanently changes things. It is hundreds of moments and thousands of choices made one after the other.

Choice requires the same strength and courage Judah displayed when he walked into school for the first time. One choice at a time to take one step at a time. I clasped my hands together and remembered Allison's words, "I think it'd be so easy in this situation to just spiral downward, and we just have to have hope. We have to be a people that have so much hope it's ridiculous. I just want to have that kind of hope. It's what's keeping us going. That's just what we have to cling to. The alternative is just to pity myself and just hate the situation I'm in and that would make things miserable. So, I choose to have hope and I choose to have a good attitude and I choose to fight."

In every story, there is a moment where hope is lost and the outcome uncertain. My story should've concluded in permanent brokenness accompanied by loss, sadness, despair, and bitterness. As I rose from the curb, I knew that was not my ending, nor Judah's, nor Allison's. Our story continues. Our story is a legacy of love and hope. I resolved to abandon pity and instead have faith, trust, thankfulness and, above all, to keep fighting for all of it.

"I can't do this without you, God," I said. "Help me be strong and courageous. Once again, I'm surrendering all to you. I'm just going to keep saying that and do my very best to follow through until my time on this earth is over."

While all stories have endings, they rarely take us to any true conclusion but, rather, the end of a single journey. This was not the end, but yet another crossroads for the journey that would begin next. Deep down I knew it wouldn't be smooth sailing. I couldn't predict or control the road ahead, but it was my choice to keep walking it or not. It would not be easy, but it would be possible because I had hope.

I looked at Future Hope Preschool and then turned my gaze up to the bright sky. Finally, I started to put one foot in front of the other but stopped briefly as I raised my index finger up for God, Allison, and the world to see. Then I quickly bent it down and up twice and pressed on.

Made in the USA
Las Vegas, NV
22 November 2024

12403959R00223